The
Secret Code
of
Success

The
Secret Code
of
Success

**7 HIDDEN STEPS TO MORE
WEALTH AND HAPPINESS**

NOAH ST. JOHN

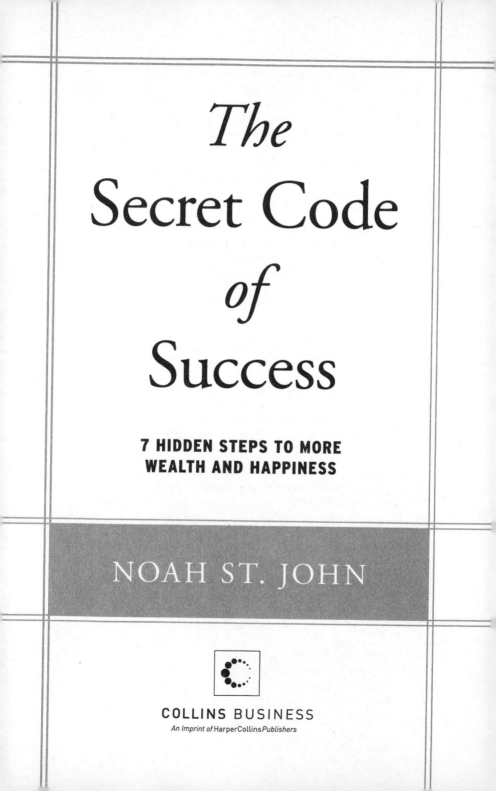

COLLINS BUSINESS
An Imprint of HarperCollins Publishers

The offer on page 219 is open to all purchasers of *The Secret Code of Success* by Noah St. John. Original proof of purchase is required. The offer is limited to the Success Camp 2.0 seminar only, and your registration for the seminar is subject to availability of space and/or changes to program schedule. Corporate or organizational purchasers may not use one book to invite more than two people. While participants will be responsible for their travel and other costs, admission to the program is complimentary. Participants in the seminars are under no additional financial obligation whatsoever to The Success Clinic or Noah St. John. The course must be completed by July 31, 2010. The value of this free admission for you and a companion is $2,990 as of February 2009.

Any mention of earnings or income should not be construed as representative of fixed or standard earnings. This book is not intended to provide personalized legal, accounting, financial, or investment advice. Readers are encouraged to seek the counsel of competent professionals with regard to such matters. The Author and Publisher specifically disclaim any liability, loss, or risk that is incurred as a consequence, directly or indirectly, of the use and application of any of the contents of this work.

Afformation/Afformations® is a registered trademark of Noah St. John and The Success Clinic of America, LLC.

FIRST EDITION

Designed by Elliott Beard

Library of Congress Cataloging-in-Publication Data
   St. John, Noah
        The secret code of success: 7 hidden steps to more wealth and happiness / by Noah St. John; foreword by Jack Canfield.
        p.   cm.
   Includes index.
   ISBN 978-0-06-171574-7 (hardcover)
   ISBN 978-0-06-176454-7 (e-book)
   1. Success in business. I. Title.
HF5386.S7595 2009
650.1—dc22

15 16 17   OV/RRD   10 9 8 7 6 5

For The Faithful

CONTENTS

ACT III-NEXT STEPS

Jack Canfield

He came up to me like anyone else. I had just flown across the country to the University of Massachusetts, where I had earned my masters degree in education, because they were presenting me with a Lifetime Achievement Award—something I wasn't all that sure about, because I still had a lot of living left to do!

When he introduced himself, he did something that thousands of other people have done before and since—said how much he enjoyed my work with *Chicken Soup for the Soul®*. But then he did something unusual, something few people had ever done before, something that got my attention. He produced what looked like a handmade book manuscript and said, "Mr. Canfield, I wonder if you could take a look at this."

He then explained that he had discovered something that would change the world of self-help as we know it . . . because he had discovered why so many smart, creative, talented people—people who'd spent tens of thousands of dollars on traditional self-help programs—are still stuck and going down the road of life with one foot on the brake!

Something about the way he spoke made me pay attention. He wasn't cocky or arrogant; rather, something about his quiet manner said that he had simply solved a problem that many, many people would like to know the solution to.

I glanced at his tape-bound book—it was literally bound with a piece of tape! It wasn't much to look at, but I noticed that he had already garnered impressive testimonials from people who were saying that his work had changed, and in some cases, saved their lives.

Maybe it was pure instinct, but something told me there was something special here. I looked up from his homemade book and said, "Yes, this looks good. I'll send it to my publisher." The look on his face was priceless. To say he was surprised would be like saying the Grand Canyon is a pretty big hole.

After Noah's first book came out, he and I continued to stay in touch. As I watched him grow and touch more and more people through his seminars and coaching programs, I felt like a proud papa—seeing my young protégé expand his reach and help tens of thousands of people around the world.

With the release of this new book, *The Secret Code of Success*, I feel that Noah is about to take the leap into true greatness. Few times in a generation does someone come along with a way of looking at a question as old as, *"Why do so many people hold themselves back from the success they're capable of?"* and come up with an answer that is at once so simple and yet so powerful.

But even more importantly, the way Noah solves this problem will allow you—no matter how rich or poor, how happy or unhappy, how stuck or successful you already are—to get your foot off the brake and allow yourself to succeed at higher levels in your life, career, and relationships than you've ever experienced before.

No matter what area of your life you want to improve—whether you want to make more money, enjoy more time off, have better relationships, improve your productivity, lose weight, or gain self-confidence—Noah will not only help you to achieve your goals . . . he'll show you how to reach them *faster, easier,* and with *far less effort* than you're spending now!

It's not often that someone you meet makes such a difference in your life, and moreover, helps you make more of a difference in the lives of others. No matter who you are or how you came to this work, the pages that follow will allow you to enter a new life.

That's why it's my great pleasure to introduce you to my colleague and friend, Noah St. John and his work, *The Secret Code of Success*.

In closing, I just have one question for you . . .

What are you waiting for?

> *All my best,*
> JACK CANFIELD
> coauthor, *Chicken Soup for the Soul*®
> and *The Success Principles*™

The "Secret" of Success in Life and Business

This is not your father's success book.

I was in Los Angeles recently having lunch with some friends who are millionaires and deca-millionaires—people worth $1 million to $10 million and up. As I looked around the table, something made me smile. I noticed that none of us looked remarkable in any way. No one was wearing an expensive suit—some of us looked like we were on our way to a pool party. We weren't discussing anything particularly deep or earth-shattering. I realized that we were really average in every visible way. You would have probably walked right by if you saw any of us on the street.

So what did this group of "regular people" do to enter the top income bracket in the world—while most continue to struggle and just get by? And more importantly: How can you learn their "secret code" so that you can enjoy this kind of success in your life and business?

In the pages that follow, you'll learn:

- What separates the top 3 percent from the rest of the world
- How to get rid of the head trash that's holding you back
- A little assumption that's costing you a fortune
- The foolproof formula for getting your foot off the brake, tailored specifically to you, so you can succeed over and over again at whatever you choose

2 Noah St. John

"WHO IS NOAH ST. JOHN AND WHY SHOULD I LISTEN TO HIM?"

You're probably asking yourself that question right now. In fact, as I'll show you later, it's impossible for you to *not* be asking yourself that question. So let me answer it right now.

As Founder and CEO of **SuccessClinic.com**, I lead an international success training company. Over the last ten years, people and organizations in over forty countries have used my methods to get better results in their lives and businesses with less time, money, and effort. I'm privileged to have thought leaders in business, sales, productivity, and human potential endorse my programs.

But things weren't always this way. Not by a long shot.

While this is kind of embarrassing to admit, I have a confession to make. When you listen to nearly every other success speaker, you'll hear stories like: He or she was a #1 salesperson in every company they were in . . . they had a paper route while still in the womb . . . or they became a millionaire while the rest of us were still playing video games.

Well, my story is just the opposite.

After skipping eighth grade, graduating second in my class, being a National Merit Scholar, and attending college on full academic scholarship, you would think I had a great future ahead of me, right?

Well, you'd be wrong. After I left college (for the first time), I became the most highly educated *under*achiever you ever saw. I found myself in a series of dead-end jobs: secretary, waiter, clerk; I sold kites, sold sweaters (not at the same store, of course); I even cleaned toilets as a housekeeper. And each job I hated more than the last.

During those long, lean years, two questions burned inside of me:

**"How could someone with so much
education have achieved so little?"**

and

**"Why are people who are *dumber*
than I am so much *richer* than I am?"**

So I did what anyone would do in that situation: I started studying the phenomenon called "success." I bought every book, listened to every CD, and went to every seminar I could. I spent lots of time, money, and energy trying to answer those two questions. It took me years and years of hard study. And after all that time, effort and expense, the question I now had was:

**"How could someone who's spent so much time and
money studying how to succeed still be so *broke*?"**

Then one night, quite by accident, I finally discovered the answer—the answer that changed my life. Not only did it explain *my* life; more importantly, my discovery has given tens of thousands of people around the world the answers in their search for Success.

And I was shocked to see that even though the answer had been right in front of me all along, *not one* of the "success gurus" I'd spent so much time, energy, and money on had ever mentioned it before.

But I'm getting ahead of myself . . .

WHY AM I SHARING THESE SECRETS?

I've already told you that I've personally helped tens of thousands of people from all walks of life to enjoy more wealth and happiness. What I didn't tell you was that it was for a much bigger purpose.

I started my company with a vision of what I wanted to create. I wanted to create a System that anyone from any background could learn, do, and teach, that would give them the skills and tools to become highly successful doing whatever they wanted to do—and I wanted to create a company that was much larger than just myself, so that we could help the millions of people who, through no fault of their own, are struggling to get ahead and succeed.

I have now achieved my vision. But, the next phase of growth for my own company is going to force me to scale back tremendously on the number of hours I am able to personally coach and mentor people. My greatest mission now is to train and grow coaches who can duplicate what I've done with my students, and empower more people than ever before to have the tools to financial freedom.

What this means is, aside from a very select group of business professionals, most people may never get the chance to work with me personally. That's why I decided it was time to get this information out there, so everyone could benefit.

ONE MORE THING

If you're looking for the same-old motivational clichés or methods you've heard a million times, you won't find them here. If you're looking for a book that tells you that you don't have to do anything to create what you really want, I'm sorry to disappoint you.

In this book, we're going to break some rules and make hamburgers out of some of self-help's most sacred cows. I'm fully aware that some of my methods may seem odd at first blush. That's the point! If you already had everything you wanted, you wouldn't need another book on how to get it, now would you?

If ever there was a time in human history when we needed to apply a new level of thinking to create a world we can all live successfully and happily in, it's now.

So let's get started!

> *To your Success,*
> NOAH ST. JOHN
> Founder, SUCCESSCLINIC.COM

ACT I

FOUNDATIONS

CHAPTER 1

What's Wrong with This Picture?

It's estimated that Americans spend $11 billion (that's a b—billion) a year on self-help products—everything from books to DVDs to diet pills—while American companies spend over $400 billion a year on professional development programs for their employees. Personally, I think those are very low estimates; especially when you consider all the weight-loss programs, exercise equipment, business books, and everything else you could put in the category of self-help.

(Yes, I know there are a lot of other, fancier terms for this: personal growth, self-improvement, professional development, etc. But for now, let's just agree to call it self-help, OK?)

Actually, I call most of this information **SHELF-help**—because that's where most of it goes—on the shelf along with all the rest of the stuff you've bought over the years. So let's just say that we are "only" spending $411 billion a year on SHELF-help products.

Now, think about this in even more concrete terms: How much money have YOU spent on SHELF-help products in the last year, two years, five years?

If you're like most of the people who come to my seminars and mentorship programs, that number is anywhere from $1,000 to $50,000 . . . and up. (I've had people come up to me in my seminars, some in tears, and tell me that what I shared with them in thirty minutes saved them over *one million dollars.*)

So heeeeeeeere's . . .

THE #1 REASON MOST PEOPLE STRUGGLE IN LIFE AND BUSINESS (AND NO, IT'S NOT WHAT YOU'VE BEEN TOLD)

Why, with all this time, money, and energy being spent on self-help, are so few people living the life they really want? Another way to ask this is:

Why are millions of people who've spent so much time and money trying to improve themselves *still* going down the road of life with one foot on the brake?

There actually is an answer to this seemingly unanswerable question. But like most vexing problems, to answer this question, we must first ask a deeper question. The deeper question we need to ask is:

WHAT CAUSES HUMAN BEHAVIOR?

While there may be many ways to answer that question, here's what I've found to be, at once, the simplest and most accurate answer to that question. It's a simple answer, because I've found (and I'm sure you have, too) that the simplest solutions tend to create the best and longest-lasting results.

THE SCALES OF SUCCESS

© AND ™ NOAH ST. JOHN

I've shown this picture to tens of thousands of people in my seminars, and I call it the **Scales of Success**.

Picture a balance, like the scales of justice you've seen in one of those courtroom TV shows. It's an instrument for determining weight that has a fulcrum at the center, from each end of which is suspended a plate.

On one plate, imagine that we have something called **Your Why-To's**. These are your internal motives or **Reasons Why** to do something. On the other plate, we have your **Why-Not-To's**—your internal **Reasons Why Not** to do something.

Let me give you an example from your own life. Why are you reading this book right now? The answer is very simple. You're reading this book because you perceive that there are more **Benefits** of reading this book (another word for Why-To's is Benefit) than **Costs** of doing so (another word for Why-Not-To's is Cost).

Your perceived Why-To's or Benefits of reading this book might include:

✔ I want to learn what the world's most successful people do, so I can do that in my own life . . .

✔ So I can stop sabotaging myself . . .

✔ So I can make more money . . .

✔ And finally get my foot off the brake . . .

✔ And this will make me happier, because I can live the life I've always wanted . . .

✔ And quit this job I hate . . .

✔ And take more vacations . . .

✔ And have better relationships . . .

✔ And lose weight . . .

✔ And find the love of my life . . .

✔ And buy a new car . . .

✔ And a new house . . .

✔ And get out of debt . . .

✔ Did I mention I'll finally get my foot off the brake?

What about your Why-Not-To's or Cost? Those might include:

✔ I have a million other things I could be doing right now.

✔ Who is this guy, anyway, and why should I listen to him?

✔ What if I get to the end and still haven't learned how to get my foot off the brake?

✔ What if it works for everyone else, but not for me?

✔ What's he trying to sell me? I've been burned before and I don't want it to happen again.

✔ Did I mention all the other things I could be doing right now?

Your mind is like an infinite weighing machine—every moment, your mind is weighing your *perceived Benefit* against your *perceived Cost* of doing any behavior or activity you can think of. Can you see that every decision we make is built upon our Why-To's and Why-Not-To's? Consider the following:

✔ Where you live
✔ What you wear
✔ What you eat (and how often you eat it)
✔ What kind of car you drive
✔ What you do for work
✔ Who you decide to marry—or not marry!
✔ What you had for breakfast this morning . . .

All of these were determined by your Why-To's and your Why-Not-To's. In fact, every decision you've ever made in your life was based on your internal Why-To's and Why-Not-To's: your reasons why you thought you should do the thing vs. the reasons not to do that thing.

BUT WHAT DOES THIS HAVE TO DO WITH SUCCESS?

"Okay, Noah," you're saying, "I can see that every decision I make is based on my Why-To's and Why-Not-To's. But what does that have to do with *success*? Are you trying to tell me, if I'm holding myself back from success, that means I *don't want* to succeed?"

I've had the privilege of working with countless thousands of people in my seminars and mentorship programs—business owners and teenagers, salespeople and accountants, employers and employees, people who work at big companies and stay-at-home moms; men, women, and children from all walks of life. And in all that time, I've never met one person who doesn't *want* to succeed.

Human beings are motivated by Success—getting, having, and keeping the things we want.

Yet we've already seen that millions of people and organizations are holding themselves back from the level of success they're perfectly capable of, even though, collectively, we're spending billions of dollars to try to fix the problem.

So, what's going on here? *There must be something hidden . . . something deeper . . . something not visible to the casual observer.*

THE HIDDEN REASON YOU'RE STUCK

Picture an iceberg. We've all heard that 90 to 95 percent of an iceberg is hidden beneath the surface of the water, while only 5 to 10 percent is visible, above the surface.

Scientists at Stanford, MIT, and other esteemed institutions have determined that the human mind operates in much the same way. Just like an iceberg, your mind is comprised of two parts: the part that's *visible* (above the surface) and the part that's *hidden* (below the surface).

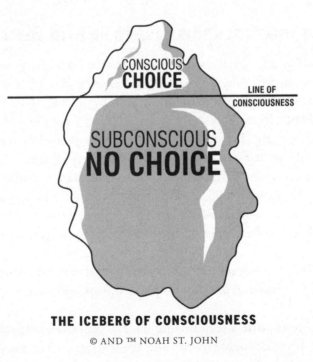

THE ICEBERG OF CONSCIOUSNESS

© AND ™ NOAH ST. JOHN

Instead of the water line, let's call the line that separates the two parts in the mind the **Line of Consciousness**. And we'll call the visible 10 percent your **Conscious Mind**, and call the hidden 90 percent the **Subconscious Mind**. Another word for conscious is *intentional*, because it represents **CHOICE**.

According to scientific research, your Conscious Mind makes up less than 10 percent of your total brain function. That means that the Subconscious Mind or *unintentional* aspect of your mind represents more than 90 percent of your total brain function.

Your subconscious is a vast collection of unintentional, habitual thoughts, behaviors, and actions. Therefore, the phrase that best describes the Subconscious Mind is **NO CHOICE**.

Look around the room you're in right now. What if I came in to the room you're in and turned out all the lights? In fact, I removed all the visible light from the room. Now it's pitch dark and you can't see a thing.

What would happen if I then asked you to rearrange the furniture? How successful would you be at rearranging the furniture in a room that's completely dark? Answer: not very. You'd bang your shins on the coffee table, fumble around, and be incapable of making even the simplest of changes.

Because you can't rearrange furniture in a place where you can't see anything, does that mean you're incapable of rearranging furniture? Of course not! You are perfectly capable of rearranging furniture—when you can see what the heck you're doing.

Your Subconscious Mind is like that completely dark room. We don't know what's in there, because we simply can't see it—it's hidden beneath the surface like the bottom 90 percent of an iceberg. And when you can't see something, it's awfully hard to change it.

Which brings us back to the original question . . .

Why are millions of people who've spent so much time and money trying to improve themselves *still stuck*?

Putting together our Scales of Success and Iceberg of Consciousness, the answer becomes stunningly simple.

Your Why-To's of Success are held in your Conscious Mind.

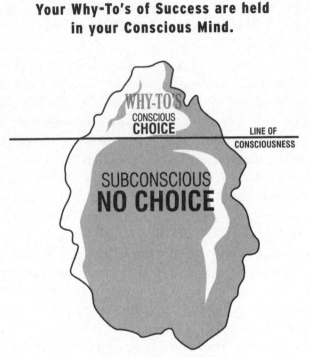

© AND ™ NOAH ST. JOHN

Everyone wants to succeed . . . on the conscious level. We all know to succeed is better than the alternative! Why do you think we're spending all this time, money, and energy trying to be more successful? So the Benefits or Why-To's of Success are held in our Conscious Mind.

But have you ever stopped to think about the Cost of actually *allowing yourself to succeed*?

I've asked this question of countless thousands of people in my seminars, and the response I get is . . . dead silence. Followed by the slightly anxious shuffling in the seats. I can practically hear people's minds whirring as they ask themselves the unexpected question: *"Gee, I've never thought of that before . . . What could be a Cost of actually allowing myself to succeed?"*

In other words, have you ever thought about the fact that, if your Why-To's of Success are held in the Conscious Mind, then . . .

Your Why-Not-To's of Success are held in your Subconscious Mind.

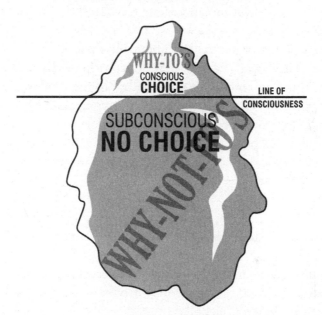

© AND ™ NOAH ST. JOHN

When I ask my audience members to give me some examples of what could possibly be a **Cost of Success**, typical answers include:

- ✔ Isn't it going to take a lot of TIME to be really successful?
- ✔ I'm too BUSY—look at my to-do list!
- ✔ I don't want the extra RESPONSIBLITY.
- ✔ What if my FAMILY doesn't approve?
- ✔ What if my SPOUSE is jealous of me?
- ✔ What if someone LAUGHS at me?
- ✔ What if my FRIENDS don't like me anymore?
- ✔ What if I succeed and can't SUSTAIN it?

✔ What if I have to spend too much time AWAY from my family?
✔ What if I go for it and LOSE it all?
✔ What if people find out I'm a FRAUD?
✔ What if . . . what if . . . what if. . .

And those are just the immediate responses! (I put that last one in there to include all ways we "what-if" ourselves.)

Did you notice something about all these Why-Not-To's of Success? They are all held in your Subconscious Mind. Meaning: No one wakes up in the morning, looks out the window and says, "Ahhh, the sun is shining, the birds are singing, and I feel great. I think I'll hold myself back from success today!"

Nor does anyone say, "I think I'll buy this book (or go to this seminar, or start this new coaching program) to learn how to sabotage myself better!"

**Every human being wants to
succeed—on the conscious level.**

But because your **Why-Not-To's of Success** are hidden in your Subconscious Mind, it's like you're driving down the road of life . . . with one foot on the brake.

WHY YOUR FOOT IS ON THE BRAKE

Let's say you've been working really hard, trying to succeed. Maybe you started a new coaching program, or went to a seminar that really pumped you up, or read a new book that really made sense to you. You began to make positive changes in your life. You followed the instructions. And guess what? *It starts to work.*

After all your hard work, focus, and money that you spent, you actually start to get what you were going after. You're moving toward the thing you want. You're making progress, making more money. You're becoming more and more successful.

Then what happens? *That's when the fear sets in!*

As crazy as it sounds, you actually start to feel the feeling known as *fear* when you start to get what you've been working so hard for. But . . .

Why would someone feel FEAR when they start to get what they WANT?

This happened because, unbeknownst to you, your Scales of Success started to tip. Your subconscious Why-Not-To's of Success—the ones you can't see, because they're hidden, remember?—started silently screaming at you: *"Hey, what do you think you're doing? You can't handle this! What if you can't keep this going? Why don't you just stop now and avoid the embarrassment later?"*

So, what do you do? What anyone would do in that situation. You do whatever it takes to *stop* feeling the fear. That's because fear is one of those emotions we humans will do just about anything to avoid. So, rather than examining why you might be feeling that feeling, *you stop doing what was working.* You slam on the brakes. You "sabotage" yourself. Because doing that feels easier than feeling the fear.

And then, you get to beat yourself up—because you can tell yourself you were right! *"See, I told you: I knew you couldn't handle it. Why even bother?"*

Sound familiar? If you are nodding your head right now, this book was written especially for you. But what went unexamined in all this is a simple fact:

A feeling is a RESULT, not a cause.

Feelings don't cause themselves. When you experience a feeling or emotion, there is something going on inside of you that caused that feeling. And what causes the so-called "fear of success" or "foot-on-the-brake syndrome"? Your hidden, subconscious Why-Not-To's of Success.

Here, then, is the bottom line:

You are not holding yourself back from Success because you don't know "how to succeed."

You are holding yourself back from the Success you are perfectly capable of, because you have more subconscious Why-Not-To's of Success than conscious Why-To's of Success.

Remember all those traditional success programs we're spending billions of dollars on? In traditional success programs, they teach you "how to succeed." And that's a good thing, right? I mean, if you want to do something, it's good to know how to do it.

And since we all want to succeed, all we'd need is to be told "how to succeed," then we'll all be successful . . . right?

Why don't you turn the page to see how that assumption is working out for you . . .

CHAPTER 2

The Little Assumption That's Costing You a Fortune

Let's say you wanted to put a nail into a wall. Do you think you could do it? Sure you could . . . if you had the right tool.

Now, let's say—because I really like you, I really believe in you, and I really want you to succeed—because of all these reasons, I went out and (with great expense and careful thought, by the way) got you a very expensive, brand new, shiny red . . .

Chainsaw.

Go ahead and put that nail in the wall.

"Okaaaaaaay," you're thinking to yourself. "He's successful, so I guess he must know what he's doing."

You start hacking away with your shiny new chainsaw.

How's it going? I ask.

"Ummm, not so good," you reply, trying to hide the big gashes you just made in the wall.

What's the matter, I ask you.

You mumble something about how you're having a tough time and struggling. So I exhort you and tell you what you should be doing to get that nail in the wall. After all, *I* was able to do it! So I give you lots of "helpful" advice, like . . .

SET YOUR GOALS!
Visualize it!
Believe in yourself!
Work smarter, not harder!
You can do it!

How's it going now?

Pretty much the same result.

Notice that I am being nice. I'm believing in you. I'm telling you things that should work. Now, what if I can see that even after all my wonderful advice, you're *still* not getting the nail in the wall.

Okay, tell you what, I say. *You can have any chainsaw you want!*

I point you to a whole rack of chainsaws—green ones, blue ones, big ones, small ones. *Pick any chainsaw you want!*

So you reluctantly try the green one because, well, maybe that will do the trick. Then the big one. Then the small one. What happens? Same result.

But how are you *feeling* right now? Are you motivated, excited, pumped up, and psyched to put that nail in the wall? Uh, not exactly. You're probably saying to yourself, "I'm never gonna get this stupid nail in the wall!"

And even if you do somehow manage to get ONE nail in, how much time, effort, and energy did it take? Aren't you feeling depressed, frustrated, angry, resentful, annoyed, irritated, exasperated, and stressed out? You probably want to do as little of this putting-the-nail-in-the-wall activity as you can.

Don't your outward ACTIONS look something like this?

- ✔ You complain to others about how tough it is to put nails in walls.
- ✔ You badmouth me, your nail-putting-in manager, behind my back.
- ✔ You make any excuse to not put nails in walls.

✔ You take it out on your kids or your spouse when you get home.

✔ Your mental and emotional health is suffering.

✔ You look for ways to medicate or "veg out" like watching TV or surfing the Internet, just to relieve the stress of putting nails in walls.

✔ You're always looking for someplace else, someplace better to work, because work is so unfulfilling.

The real problem is NOT that you can't do the job.

The real problem is that you are beating yourself up for not being able to do a job . . . When you have been given a tool that is COMPLETELY WRONG for the job you're trying to do.

The only solutions you have been offered are simply the same tools with different packaging! So even though it would appear that putting a nail into a wall is an easy job, if you have never been given the right tool, it will continue to be very, very difficult.

Now, is there anything wrong with a chainsaw? Of course not! Chainsaws are very useful tools . . . when you want to cut down a tree. But when you want to put a nail in a wall, they're not very useful at all.

How many times have you seen the equivalent of what I've just shown you in your life, career, or company? When I ask that question in my seminars, nearly every hand goes up. We've all seen examples of people who had all the talent, intelligence, and motivation in the world, who were asked to "put nails in walls" and given a "chainsaw." Here's just a smidgen of the figures:

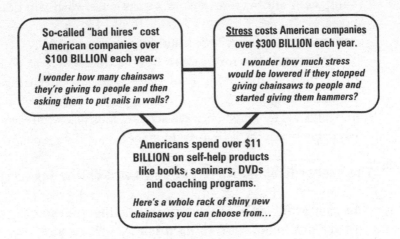

The problem is not bad hires, stress, or over-consumption. The problem is that we've been searching for "the hammer" to put that nail in the wall . . . but all we've been given are chainsaws.

THE ASSUMPTION

We all know people who've spent lots of time, money, and energy on traditional success programs, who are still holding themselves back from the success they're perfectly capable of. (Hmmm, maybe you know someone like that . . . *intimately?)* But how and why could this happen?

In traditional success programs, we have been taught "how to succeed"—what I call the **How-To's of Success**. This happened because traditional success teachers assumed that all we'd need is to be shown how to succeed, and then, of course, we'd succeed.

They taught us the How-To's of Success because of a single assumption—an assumption that turned out to be false. They made this assumption without even thinking about it, because it was totally illogical to think otherwise. This single assumption, however, is costing you a fortune right now.

Traditional success programs taught us the How-To's of Success, because traditional teachers assumed that you and I had more Why-To's of Success than Why-Not-To's of Success.

They actually had it *half* right. Everyone *does* have more Why-To's of Success—but only on the conscious level. That's why we keep spending billions of dollars on all these success programs!

Remember our iceberg? Just because you can't see your Why-Not-To's of Success doesn't mean they're not there. They're there all right, hidden in the subconscious, where they keep you held back from the very thing you want most. *But...*

THAT'S NOT EVEN THE MOST AMAZING PART (THIS IS)

Here is the most amazing part about all this—and it represents the key to your freedom, success, and fulfillment:

You can never solve a Why-To problem with a How-To solution.

Read that sentence again. Because, if you are holding yourself back from success, you don't have a How-To problem. You have a Why-To/Why-Not-To problem. *You can never solve a Why-To problem with a How-To solution.*

That single sentence explains why:

- Americans spend billions of dollars a year on self-help programs, yet most remain stuck.
- You have spent thousands, maybe tens of thousands of dollars, on SHELF-help programs . . . and still have your foot on the brake.

- The world's most successful people, the ones teaching all those "how-to succeed" programs, can never tell you how to get your foot off the brake . . . because they are *unconscious* at *allowing* themselves to succeed.

And it also explains why the people you'll meet in the pages that follow—the people who've taken the Steps revealed in this book—have:

- ✔ Doubled, tripled, even quintupled their income in less than a year
- ✔ Lost twenty pounds in sixty days without stress or dieting
- ✔ Converted their annual income into their monthly income— even their *weekly* income
- ✔ Overcome the darkest moments of despair and helplessness to achieve greatness and find fulfillment

These are just some of the remarkable results my Students have seen in their lives, careers, and relationships. And you can do it, too—provided you follow *The Secret Code of Success*.

Oh, there's one more thing I wanted to show you . . .

THE FOUR STEPS OF TRADITIONAL SUCCESS PROGRAMS

I'm about to save you a ton of money, years of your life, and lots of frustration. How? By giving you the four steps of every traditional "how to succeed" program. Here they are:

1. **Set your goals** (Know what you want)

2. **Do something** (Take action toward your goals)

3. **Evaluate** (Am I getting closer to my goals or not?)

4. **Try again** (Adjust your approach until you reach your goals)

If you've ever experienced a self-help book, speech, or seminar, you've probably heard those same four steps over and over, packaged in different ways. And it sounds great, doesn't it? You knew this already, didn't you?

So you have everything you want, right?

(Sound of crickets chirping)

What was that?

You *don't* have everything you want? Well, what's wrong with you?

Oh. You must not be *motivated* enough.

Or you just don't *work hard* enough.

Or you're not *intelligent* enough.

Or maybe you're just *incapable* of succeeding.

Wait a minute! Are you kidding me?! Delete those sentences. After all, we can't all be that stupid.

THE FOUR STEPS OF THE REAL WORLD

Just like traditional success programs have given us the same four steps, there are also four steps in *the real world*—that would be like, uh, planet Earth. Here are the four basic steps I have observed about the real world (see if you've found these to be true, too):

1. **The Fog** (We don't know what we really want)

2. **Treadmilling** (We're really really busy, but getting nowhere)

3. **Feel Like a Failure** (We compare ourselves to everyone else and come up short)

4. **Try Again** (We keep trying and hoping things will be different)

In the first step, we don't really know what we want . . . or we don't know what we *really* want . . . or we don't *believe* we can have what we really want . . . or we *fear*, "What will so-and-so say if I actually get what I really want?" . . . or we *think*, "I don't think I'll ever get what I really want" . . . or "What if I get what I really want and then I'm still not happy?" . . . or . . .

Get it? We have a **Fog**.

In the second step, we are **Treadmilling**. Ever been on a treadmill? You're working really, really hard and getting . . . nowhere!

Look at my to-do list! I'm busy busy busy . . . but this view sure looks the same!

And sometimes that treadmill is going uphill—*Whew! I'm working working working, busy busy busy!* But things still haven't changed.

Treadmilling. Are you with me here?

Now we get to the critical third step, **Feel Like a Failure**. Now, watch this. There is an amazing parallel between what they've been teaching us in traditional success programs, and what we find in the real world:

- In traditional success programs, they said to *set your goals*. Well, we don't really know what we want, so we've got a *Fog*.
- Then they told us to *do something*. Well, we're really really busy, aren't we? So we're *Treadmilling*.
- Then they told us to *evaluate* our progress. Well, what's our *subconscious evaluation* of our own progress?

You got it—we feel like a failure. We feel like everyone else is doing better than we are. We wonder why we've spent all that time, money, and energy on all these self-help programs . . . and we're still stuck.

We look at all the exercise equipment, money-making schemes, diet pills, relationship advice, all the SHELF-help products and programs we've invested in—then look at where we are in life and how we feel stuck—and inside, we feel like a failure.

Boy, did I spend years of my life in this step. *I don't want you to spend one more minute there.*

And yet, even with all that—all the years of frustration and tens of thousands of dollars we've spent (with not much to show for it) . . . even with all that, we still do Step 4, and **Try Again**.

You see, you *are* motivated. You *do* want to succeed. You *have* kept trying, even though you may have "failed" in the past. You really deserve a medal for continuing to press on, even in the face of not getting the results you've wanted . . . even though you've never been given the right tool to do the job!

Now, are you ready for the biggest shock of all? Here it is:

If you want to reach your full potential, you don't need any more "how to succeed" information.

I know that sounds crazy, even blasphemous to those people who've spent tons of money on every "how to succeed" program out there. But that's the very point. You've spent all that time, money, and energy . . . and you're still not where you want to be . . . and your foot's still on the brake.

That's why I'm not going to teach you "how to succeed"—not because I don't want to, but *because I don't have to.* You've been told all you need to know about "how to succeed."

Now it's time that you *allow yourself to succeed* to your full potential. It's time to get your foot off the brake in your life, career, and relationships for good. And I'm going to show you exactly how to do that . . .

A QUICK RECAP

1. There is a secret to becoming highly successful. The secret is: There is a massive, fundamental difference between "how to succeed" and *how to let yourself succeed.* The problem is, the people who are unconscious at letting themselves succeed can't tell you what it is—for the precise reason that they are doing it *unconsciously.*

2. What really causes human behavior is your internal Why-To's and Why-Not-To's—the reasons *you perceive* why to do something or not do it.

3. Therefore, the reason you're holding yourself back from success has nothing to do with your How-To's of Success. It has to do with uncovering your subconscious Why-Not-To's of *allowing yourself* to be truly successful.

4. Holding yourself back from success is a Why-To/Why-Not-To problem. ***You can never solve a Why-To problem with a How-To solution.***

5. Traditional success programs have taught us the How-To's of Success. While there's nothing wrong with this, trying to get your foot off the brake using traditional "how-to" methods is like trying to put a nail into a wall using a chainsaw.

6. This simple fact explains why millions of people and organizations are spending billions of dollars every year on every "how to succeed" program out there . . . yet most people still feel stuck.

7. If you want to get your foot off the brake for good, stop spending your hard-earned money on more How-To's of Success. Instead, focus on your internal Why-To's and Why-Not-To's of Success, and take the appropriate steps to restore the proper balance. Why? Because using the right tool—the steps provided in this book—will produce greater results faster, easier, and with less effort than you're spending now.

CHAPTER 3

The Secret Code Revealed

Have you ever noticed that sometimes, a single idea can change the entire course of your life? On the night of October 20, 1997, I "accidentally" made a discovery that did that to me. Since then, tens of thousands of people around the world have used what I discovered that night to change their lives, too.

On that fateful fall night, I was attending a seminar on eating disorders. Remember how I told you I worked in a series of jobs after my first time in college? One of those jobs was as a professional ballet dancer. After performing with several professional ballet companies across the country, I decided to go back to college to finish my degree in religious studies.

On the morning of my discovery, I saw a sign in a local bookstore for a seminar on eating disorders to be held that night. Even though I never had suffered from an eating disorder, many of my friends and colleagues had. So I decided to attend the seminar to learn why people would do this to themselves.

At the seminar, the speaker described why so many smart, creative, talented, sensitive people—mostly young women—developed eating disorders and would starve themselves. She said that it was not a matter of nutrition or of needing to teach them which foods to eat. Having worked with thousands of people at her clinic, the speaker concluded that the person suffering from an eating disorder was holding *a desire to not be here on Earth.* In essence, she wanted to *disappear*—to *punish herself* because of a deeply negative self-image.

As the speaker continued to describe people who starve themselves, I noticed something I never expected—she was describing *me* to a tee. She said that people who starve themselves are smart, creative, talented, and motivated. Check, check, check, and check. She said they're usually straight-A students and overachievers in school. Check. She said they're highly sensitive to the needs of others, and put other people's needs and feelings ahead of their own. Check and check.

Then, she said that these individuals settle for crumbs while others around them are eating fully. While I knew this was not true in relation to food (I love food and enjoy eating), I thought to myself, "What if we extrapolate and see that I am settling for *the crumbs of life*—while I constantly help others get ahead, even at my own expense?"

Wait a minute, I thought to myself. *I've been settling for crumbs my whole life.*

It was at that moment that lightning struck—and my life made sense for the very first time.

THE STARVATION OF SUCCESS

When we talk about starvation, or eating disorders like anorexia and bulimia, we're normally referring to behavior relating to food. For example, when someone is said to have the condition called *anorexia*, we are typically describing a behavior pattern marked by an aversion to or *pushing away* of food. When someone has *bulimia*, it typically means behavior characterized by the *bingeing and purging* of food (gorging on food and then inducing vomiting).

Up until that moment, no one had ever thought that starvation behaviors could be related to anything but food. I suppose the assumption was that other than food, what could human beings consume (and therefore starve ourselves of)?

But at the moment I became aware that I was settling for *the crumbs of life*, I realized that there was something else we humans could starve themselves of, and this previously unrecognized method of starvation was affecting tens of millions of people. What no one had considered before was that human beings could *starve ourselves of success*.

Think about this for a moment. Women, since the beginning of human history, have been taught that their worth comes from their physical bodies. While it is totally politically incorrect to say this, the fact remains that women, for most of the history of civilization, were treated like possessions to be sold and acquired for the purposes of marriage and procreation.

Make no mistake about it: *A woman's worth does not come from her body!* However, since the beginning of time, female human beings have been *told* or *taught*—implicitly and explicitly—that their worth stems from their physical bodies.

So, let's say you have a human being who has been *told* since the beginning of time that her worth comes from her physical body (even though it isn't true, it's what she's been *taught*). Let's further say that this person develops really low self-esteem and a very low sense of self-worth. So now you have a person who's been told that her worth comes from her physical body . . . and you add to that a very low sense of self-worth . . .

Doesn't it make sense that that person will *punish* that part of herself that she was *told* her worth comes from—namely, her physical body? And if you are going to unconsciously punish your physical body, doesn't it make sense that you are going to *starve yourself of food*?

I have just shown you, in five sentences, what causes a person to develop an eating disorder.

Now, I realize that no woman reading this book was told in a literal sense "your worth comes from your physical body." But if you happen to live on the planet Earth and are female, it's nearly impossible for this belief to not have affected you—simply because it's been around for so many centuries. Which leads us to . . .

THE OTHER SEX

That would be, men.

Where have *men* been taught their worth comes from? Men, since the beginning of human history, have been *taught* or *told* that their worth comes from their possessions, titles, job, net worth, holdings, size of bank account—what I call their *material bodies* (as opposed to their *physical bodies*).

While it is also completely politically incorrect to say this, the fact remains that men have been judged almost solely on what they possess or are capable of earning—bringing home the bacon. Of course, this is not where a man's worth comes from—it is just what men have been *told* or *taught* their worth comes from.

So, what if you have a human being who has been *told* since the beginning of time that his worth comes from . . . not his physical body, but his material body (even though this isn't true, it's what he's been *taught*). Let's further assume that this person develops a really negative self-image. Now you have a person who's been *told* that his worth comes from his material body . . . and you add to that a very low sense of self-worth . . .

Doesn't it make sense that he will punish that part of himself that he was *told* his worth comes from—namely, his material body? And if you are going to unconsciously punish your material body, doesn't it make sense that you are going to *starve yourself of success*?

THE CONDITION WITH NO NAME

I have just shown you what causes something you've probably never thought about before, because it never had a name before, because no one had ever realized its existence before. And it's called a **success disorder**.

What is a success disorder? It's what happens when a person develops a deeply negative self-belief—what I call your **head trash**—and unconsciously develops a pattern of behavior marked by *an aversion to or pushing away of success*.

I know this sounds crazy—except to the tens of millions of us who have been doing it our whole lives without knowing it. At 8:20 p.m. on October 20, 1997, I became the first person to realize the existence of a condition that I named **success anorexia.**

Because of this, I also realized that *starvation* could be related to something other than food—and that tens of millions of people around the world were unknowingly *starving ourselves of success*—but had no idea that's what we were doing, let alone how to fix the problem.

That's when I knew I had to get this information out to the millions of people just like me—people who were unknowingly pushing away the success we were perfectly capable of achieving.

And that's the moment *The Secret Code of Success* was born.

BONUS PRESSURES FOR WOMEN

Did you notice something about the examples in the previous section? I showed you why people who starve themselves of food tend to be females, while people who starve themselves of success tend to be males. But what if you're a *woman* who's starving yourself of *success*? How could that happen?

The answer is simple: Over the last fifty years, women have entered the workplace in unprecedented numbers. In fact, women now outnumber men in the workforce, and research shows that women are starting new businesses at a higher rate than men.

Guess what this means for today's modern woman? In addition to being told that their worth comes from their *physical* bodies, they're now being told that their worth comes from their *material* bodies!

This means that women now face the dual pressures of having to "look perfect" (*physical* body pressure—the traditional female measuring stick) while also having to have "the perfect career" and "bring home the bacon" (*material* body pressure—the traditional male measuring stick).

Keep in mind that none of these pressures are spoken of in polite company. They are lurking beneath the surface, never addressed in the open . . . but always there, affecting millions of women and men all over the world—although very few are consciously aware of it.

The bottom line is that today's modern woman can be starving herself of food *and* success! Many of my female Students have come to me for help because they were holding themselves back from success, and then told me that they were anorexic or bulimic at one time in their lives. Even though you may never have suffered from an eating disorder, if you are a woman, you too are probably facing these unspoken pressures of modern life.

THE TWO TRUTHS

Alex Mandossian, founder of Heritage House Publishing and one of my first mentors, has often said there are two truths in life:

1. Everyone has potential.

2. No one has reached it yet.

But why is that? After working with countless thousands of people in my seminars and mentorship programs, I've come to realize that while we human beings fear *not being* Who We Really Are, what we tend to fear even more is *being* Who We Really Are.

My friend Neale Donald Walsch, author of the *Conversations with God* series, put it elegantly when he said, "Since the beginning of time, all we have wanted is to love and be loved. And since the beginning of time, all we have stopped from happening is to love and be loved."

That's why the purpose of this book is to give you permission to be Who You Really Are—*permission to succeed*. How can you gain that permission if you don't already have it?

Simple. All you have to do is follow the secret code that the world's rich, happy people are unconsciously following, that they don't even know they're following, and that they can't tell you about—not because they don't want to, but because success has become as unconscious for them as breathing or driving a car is for the rest of us.

That's when you'll finally discover how amazing it is to live your life without your foot on the brake . . .

MEET THE THREE PERCENTERS

I want to introduce you to a very special group of people. Actually, you've seen these people on TV or in the movies; and you've certainly seen them onstage, winning award after award at your company's annual convention.

These are the world's most successful people. They have most of the wealth, happiness, joy, peace, health, and loving relationships—in other words, they have most of what we human beings want as we go through this journey called Life.

Please note: In this book, I am talking about fulfilled, wealthy people—what I call being happy and rich. There are lots of people with lots of money who are unhappy, and people who are broke but happy (although not many of those). But I've observed that while most people believe you can either be happy or rich, there's a small percentage of people who realize you can be both.

I call these special people the **Three Percenters.** Why? Well, you've heard of the 80/20 Rule (also known as *Pareto's Principle*)—that 80 percent of your results flow from 20 percent of your efforts. But in today's society, we seem to have what I call the **97/3 Rule**—that about 3 percent of the population holds most of the world's great wealth, while most of the remaining 97 percent struggle just to get by.

While these may not be precise, hard and fast numbers, look around and you can verify them for yourself. Look around your company and you'll see that the same one, two, or five sales-people always, *always* win the top awards—while the rest never do. Look around your personal relationships and notice that a tiny minority of couples ever stays *happily* married; the rest just stay married. Look around the mall and notice how many people are in shape and healthy . . . and how many are not. Look around the world and see that only a small percentage of the world's population are Haves, and the rest are Have-Nots (or at least Have-Not-Much).

Well, you may say, it's just not fair. Money, wealth, health, happiness—these should be given equally to all people. You're right, they should—and indeed, they are. It's just that few people ever choose to take them and make correct use of them.

These "lucky" few are the Three Percenters. But here's their big "secret":

You can be a Three Percenter, too . . .
but only if you learn and follow their secret code.

JUST ONE THING

"Ah-ha," I can hear you saying. "I *knew* there was a catch!"

Yep, there's a catch all right.

If you believe that most of the wealth, health, happiness, joy, love, opportunity—in short, all of the things we humans want—is held by 3 percent of the world's population, you need to realize that it is not actually "held" anywhere. No one can keep love, money, or opportunity away from you, any more than someone can stop you from reaching your full potential.

But here's the amazing, counterintuitive thing about the Three Percenters: *They can't really tell you how they got there!*

Have you ever heard a speech, read a book, or gone to a seminar given by a Three Percenter? Yes, you have—you just didn't realize it. Remember the last seminar you went to on self-improvement? The last book on how to increase your sales or grow your business? That speech given by the mega-rich investor?

That seminar, book or speech was almost certainly given by someone who was unconsciously competent at allowing themselves to succeed. In other words, a Three Percenter.

What do I mean by *unconsciously competent at allowing yourself to succeed*? When you are trying to do something new—walk, tie your shoes, drive a car, make a million dollars, make 100 million dollars—the four levels of competency you go through are:

1. *Unconscious incompetence*: you don't know that you don't know

2. *Conscious incompetence:* you know that you don't know

3. *Conscious competence:* you know that you know

4. *Unconscious competence*: you do it without conscious thought

Think about driving a car. Remember the very first time you were in a car when you were a little kid? I sure don't. I don't remember thinking, "Gee, when I'm big and tall and I can reach the pedals with my little feet, I wonder what it's going to feel like to drive this . . . what do they call it again?"

The point is, you were driven around (unless your parents let you drive when you were an infant, in which case we really need to talk), and the thought of driving a car never entered your mind. Why would it? You were a kid, for crying out loud!

Then, when you got to the age of, let's say, twelve, you started to think, "Hey, these goofy adults have these weird things called *cars* and they let you go where you want to when you want to . . . and all

I have is a bike and they won't let me ride my bike on the highway so I can't get very far . . . I think I want a car!"

And your next thought was, "How the heck am I going to do that?"

Then you had to wait another three or four years before they let you take driver's ed . . . and then you thought, "This is more like it! Now I can go where I want when I want, and no one can tell me what to do!" Well, you weren't exactly right about that particular thought, but still—you were on your way.

And today? You're in your car/truck/minivan/hybrid, talking on the phone, sipping coffee, putting on your makeup, looking at the drivers around you, finding a good radio station, thinking about your next meeting, getting one kid to stop torturing the other or so help me I'll pull this car over . . . and, oh yeah, driving. After all those years and years of waiting and waiting and waiting, you have become *unconscious* at driving a car.

When you're driving your car today, do you ever think about all those years and years of waiting and waiting and waiting? Of course not! Until I just brought it up, when was the last time you thought about all those long, long years of waiting until you could drive a car? Like, never?

Exactly.

LEARNING FROM UNCONSCIOUS PEOPLE

Let's go back to our Three Percenters—the people who have what the rest of the world wants. Many of these Three Percenters realized that they could help people (and make a lot of money) by teaching other people the so-called "secrets of success." In other words, "how I got here."

I'm sure most of them do this because they really want to help people. And they do mean well. There's only one problem . . .

**When you are unconsciously competent
at something, you often don't know how
you are really doing that thing.**

For example, when I worked as a professional ballet dancer, I was good, but never the lead dancer. I sweated, worked my butt off, and tried harder than anyone else, but just wasn't as proficient as the lead guys. Sometimes when I was having trouble with a particular step, I would notice who was doing it naturally and ask them to show me how to do it. And they would say something like, "Just do it . . . turn your head . . . just spin . . ." or something totally not helpful at all!

One day, I realized I wasn't getting anywhere and asked one of the older members of the company to help me. He wasn't tallest or strongest, but he was the best *teacher*, because he patiently showed me how to do the steps by breaking them down until I had mastered them. He was definitely *not* a Natural, and neither was I—but while the Naturals were no help at all, this man helped me more than any of them, because he showed me step-by-step what I needed to do.

It is the same way with the phenomenon called Success. Almost all of the books, speeches, and seminars you see on "how to succeed" are being given by Three Percenters—the **Naturals at Success**. I'm not suggesting that Naturals don't work hard or haven't made sacrifices to get where they are; Naturals have to work hard, just like the rest of us. But my point is this:

**The true causes of success are often hidden
and counterintuitive, even—especially!—to
those who are Naturals at Success.**

There is something the Naturals (the Three Percenters) are doing that they don't know they're doing. And no matter how many times they tell you their "secrets of success," they can't tell you something they're not consciously aware of. It's like saying to a fish, "So, tell me about water!"

That's why it took a highly educated underachiever like me—and an unexpected twist of fate—to realize that the Three Percenters were living by a code they weren't consciously aware of. If only the rest of us could follow it . . .

BEING AND DOING

The Secret Code of Success is *a way of life* that involves *being* and *doing*. It's a code of living, not like a code you use to open a safe.

The way of *Being* is first, to discover Who You Really Are, and the way of *Doing* is to act in accord with Who You Really Are. Together, this Being and Doing will allow you to succeed to your fullest potential. How do we do that? By following the seven Steps of *The Secret Code of Success*.

You may be wondering why *The Secret Code of Success* is a "secret" in the first place. Why doesn't *everyone* know about this Code? I believe it's been a secret for this long for two main reasons:

1. Because the Three Percenters themselves don't know it exists, since they're unconscious of the fact that they're following it in the first place.

2. Because the Code cannot be found in the conscious world of everyday demands and pressures, but lies within and requires a new way of looking at the phenomenon called Success.

The Secret Code of Success reveals what the Three Percenters do unconsciously *that they could never tell you,* because they are unconsciously competent at allowing themselves to succeed.

WHY SHOULD I FOLLOW THE CODE, ANYWAY?

You may be asking yourself that question right now. In fact, it's impossible for your brain to *not* be asking that question! (Remember our Scales of Success?) So let's put our cards on the table right now.

In working with tens of thousands of people in my seminars and private mentorship programs, here are the seven main Benefits (Why-To's) that I have observed my Students experience once they begin to start living the Code:

1. You will get rid of the head trash that's holding you back from success.

2. You will allow yourself to make more money.

3. Your sales/recruiting efforts will improve.

4. You will enjoy improved relationships with yourself and with others.

5. Your self-confidence will increase naturally.

6. You will experience enhanced feelings of happiness, connection, joy, enthusiasm, and love.

7. You will begin to know and live your purpose on Earth.

NO MORE HEAD TRASH

When you follow the Code, the big Benefit you will experience (and the big promise of this book) is that you will eliminate the *causes* of self-sabotage, the fear of success, and the foot on the brake syndrome. I want you to understand something absolutely key here. Self-destructive behaviors that hold you back from success are precisely that: behaviors.

A **behavior** is something you do that is caused by something else. You do not do anything without a reason. *The true cause of all human behavior is your Why-To's and your Why-Not-To's.* This leads us to one of the fundamental truths in my approach, which itself represents a major shift in the field of self-improvement:

You cannot change your behavior at the level of behavior.

Let me give you an example. If you're old enough to read this book, you probably take a shower or bath every day before going to work, to school, or starting your day. Why? Because you wouldn't like the way you felt if you didn't!

Now, you could, if you wanted to, not bathe before going to work. Why don't you do that? It's probably never even occurred to you to even ask the question. Why *wouldn't* you?

Exactly. The reason you bathe to start your day is because it's an unconscious habit. In fact, until this moment, it's probably never occurred to you to not do it, because you've been doing it for so long.

Now, *could you* go to work without bathing? Sure, you could. So why don't you? Because you wouldn't like the results, both from yourself and the not-very-approving looks from your coworkers.

So, you have all the Why-To's of bathing and all the Why-Not-To's of not bathing. Those two forces together produce the very powerful—and unconscious—Why-To's of bathe-before-work.

But we've just determined that, if you wanted to, you could go to work without bathing. (By the way, I don't recommend this, and your co-workers probably wouldn't appreciate it, either.) In other words, you have the How-To's of not-bathing-before-work.

However, because your Why-To's outweigh your Why-Not-To's, you are firmly in the camp of bathe-before-work. That's why you can know how to do something, and never let yourself do it.

And that's why Why-To's will always, always, *always* trump How-To's.

MOVING BEYOND BEHAVIOR

We've already seen that holding yourself back from success is a Why-To/Why-Not-To problem, and that you can never solve a Why-To problem with a How-To solution. We've also seen that since traditional success programs are focused on the How-To's of Success, using those programs to get your foot off the brake is like trying to put a nail into a wall using a chainsaw.

Before *The Secret Code of Success*, all attempts to fix the age-old question of "how to get your foot off the brake" have been at the level of behavior. The Three Percenters told us to *think positive, set your goals,* and *just do it* (the How-To's of Success). While these exhortations are not wrong any more than a chainsaw is wrong, the problem is that these are all *behaviors.* And as we've just seen with the bathe-before-work example, you cannot solve a behavior problem *at the level of behavior.* You must go beneath your behavior to the hidden Why-To's and your Why-Not-To's of your behavior.

That's what *The Secret Code of Success* is all about. That is the question the Three Percenters have unconsciously answered for themselves, which is exactly why they allow themselves to succeed and don't have their foot on the brake.

And that's the secret that the rest of us can now share in—as long as we follow the Code.

What's truly amazing about the Code is that *you cannot hold yourself back from Success if you simply do the seven Code Steps.* Now, if you don't do the seven Code Steps, I can't make any promises. Actually, I can make one promise: you'll still have your foot on the brake!

The System I teach is not magic. You can't just read this book, put it down and say, "Okay, I'm fixed!" any more than you can read a book about cleaning your office and expect it to happen all by itself (would be nice, though, wouldn't it?).

You must TAKE ACTION. The point is, if you simply do the seven Steps of the Code, it is actually not possible to hold yourself back from success. Follow the Code, and you will eliminate self-sabotage for good. I'm not saying this to make you feel good; what I'm telling you is based on my experience with tens of thousands of grateful Students in my seminars and mentorship programs.

Now that you know what you're going to get as a result of following the Code, and that you must TAKE ACTION to get those Benefits, it's time to reveal The seven Steps of *The Secret Code of Success.*

THE PERMISSION PYRAMID™

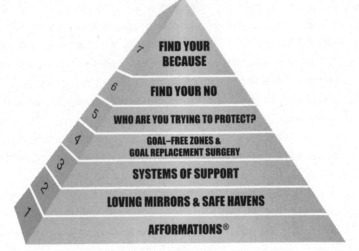

These seven Steps are simple to understand, but require effort to execute. Beginning with Step 1, you will begin to move up the Permission Pyramid, reprogramming your Subconscious Mind so that your Why-Not-To's are no longer holding you back from more wealth and happiness.

Step 1 is **Afformations**. No, that's not a misprint. **Afformations** are empowering *questions* (NOT affirmations) that immediately change your subconscious thought patterns from negative to positive. Using Afformations instead of affirmations, you'll be able to manifest the things you want twice as fast with half the effort.

In Step 2, **Loving Mirrors and Safe Havens**, you'll learn how to gain unconditional support for your life, career, and relationships. This is the primary unconscious Step that Three Percenters use—and without it, you can never reach your full potential.

Step 3 is **Systems of Support.** Just like your house or your body, your life and your business have essential Systems that must function properly to create maximum success with minimum effort. The Three Percenters are using these five essential Systems of Support without even knowing it; follow this Step and you can, too.

Step 4 deals with the sticky question of where goals fit into your life. In **Goal-Free Zones**, you'll learn the necessity of unplugging to re-energize and revitalize yourself daily. In **Goal Replacement Surgery,** you'll discover if your stated goals are really yours or if they're someone else's that you've internalized.

Step 5 is a question you've probably never asked before: "**Who Am I Trying to Protect, Punish or Please?**" Many people have, upon taking this Step, realized that they had been unconsciously holding themselves back to protect or punish someone else. Once freed from those hidden blocks, they've seen incredible increases in both income and peace of mind very quickly.

Step 6 is to **Find Your No**. Many people have lost their No— that is, lost their ability to say no to others. When you lose your No, you become a doormat to the agendas of others, which means your dreams and aspirations are put aside. I'll show you some simple but powerful ways to Find Your No so that your dreams become just as important as anyone else's.

Finally, Step 7, **Find Your Because**, deals with your mission, your purpose on Earth—your Ultimate Why-To. Most people don't know why they're here on Earth, and this not-knowing leads to feelings from frustration, anger, and boredom to depression and the deepest depths of despair. When you Find Your Because and complete all seven Steps, you will become a Three Percenter—

because you will be one of the tiny percentage of human beings who not only knows their purpose, but has the tools to make the world a better place for themselves and everyone else.

Are you ready to get your foot off the brake and fly?

ACT II

THE CODE

CHAPTER 4

Step 1: Afformations

**Every sentence I utter must be understood
not as an affirmation, but as a question.**

—NIELS BOHR, NOBEL PRIZE-WINNING PHYSICIST

April 1997. A crisp spring morning like any other in New England.
I was living in a dorm room at the college where I was a religious
studies major. The dorm room itself was sizable enough, in that,
simply by standing in the middle of the room, you could touch the
walls on both sides.

It was the morning of The Shower That Changed My Life.

The night before, I'd been looking around my diminutive dorm room and realized that I had posted lots of sayings or *affirmations* around the room to make myself feel better. If you've read a self-help book or been to a success seminar in the last forty years, chances are you've heard of affirmations. Why? Because nearly every traditional success teacher tells you to use them!

As you know, an affirmation is *a statement of something you want to be true in your life.* So, examples of traditional affirmations are, *"I am happy, healthy, and wealthy," "I am good enough,"* and *"I am rich."* Now, since I'd spent so much time and money studying traditional success literature, and since every traditional success teacher tells you to use them, I'd been writing and saying affirmations for years.

But, for some reason, my life still sucked.

THE SHOWER THAT CHANGED MY LIFE

That morning in The Shower, my mind wandered. I began asking simple but profound questions about the nature of life—my life. Questions like:

"If I've been doing what they told me to do, and saying these affirmations for so many years, how come my life still sucks?" And:

"If I've been saying these positive statements to myself for years, how come I still don't feel good about myself?" And:

"There must be a better way to get me to believe something good about myself. But what is it?"

That's when it hit me. (No, not the soap.)

I realized that the human brain is always asking and searching for answers to *questions.* In that moment, I realized that *thought itself is the process of asking and searching for the answers to questions.*

If that's true, I reasoned, then a simple question formed naturally in my mind—The Question That Changed Everything:

**"If human thought is the process of asking
and searching for answers to *questions* . . .**

**Why are we going around making *statements*
that we DON'T BELIEVE?"**

I couldn't think of a good answer to that question.

That's when everything changed for me—and for my tens of thousands of Students (who call themselves The Faithful) around the globe who've since learned how to apply what I discovered in The Shower.

Let me show you what I mean . . .

WHY AFFIRMATIONS DON'T WORK
AS ADVERTISED

We all know that an affirmation is *a statement of something you want to be true.* So an example of a traditional affirmation might be: *"I am rich."*

All right, let's try it.

Say to yourself right now, *"I am rich."*

Try it again. *"I am rich."*

Did you hear what just happened in your mind?

A voice . . . a voice that said something like:

"Yeah, right!"

Let me ask you a question. Tell the truth. Do you honestly believe your own affirmations—or do you doubt them?

The plain and simple truth is that most of us doubt our own affirmations. Why? *Because we're trying to convince ourselves of something, and our minds don't believe that it's true.*

Now, traditional success teachers (most of whom, remember, are unconscious at allowing themselves to succeed) realized that you may not believe your affirmations. So they told you, with good intentions, that all you had to do was repeat your affirmations a thousand . . . er, million . . . uh, kajillion times until you eventually, um, believe them.

Let's say you realized you were holding onto negative thoughts (for example, *"I'm poor, I'm lonely, I don't have enough"*). You decided you wanted something better . . . said positive affirmations (for example, *"I am rich, I'm happy, I have enough"*) . . . and then had . . .

Absolutely nothing happen?

Me too. And about a gazillion other people. Hey, we were only given chainsaws, so what else were we supposed to use?

But why? Why didn't affirmations work for most of us? If it were as easy as the traditional teachers said, why did nothing happen for the rest of us? Were we simply incapable of thinking a positive thought? Were we not *smart enough, motivated enough, educated enough* . . . or did we just not try *hard enough?*

The answer is: *none of these.*

The answer is: You were given the wrong tool to do the job.

You were told you could change your mind using *statements* . . . when your mind responds naturally to *questions.*

You were told you could overcome negative beliefs using *statements* . . . when it's so much easier to overcome them using *questions.*

You were told to *tell* . . . when you should have been shown how to *ask.*

What in the world do I mean?

WHAT EVERY PROBLEM YOU'LL EVER FACE REALLY IS

We typically fear, try to avoid, ignore, or get away from problems. But really, a problem is simply *a question that hasn't been answered yet.*

Any problem, from the trivial to the tremendous, is really a question searching for an answer. Here are a few serious global problems and their associated questions:

Global warming: "How can we stop destroying the Earth and still live the lives we want?"

Poverty: "How can we equally distribute the wealth of the world so that people don't have to go without the basic necessities of life?"

Unemployment: "How can we get everyone working in jobs that produce wealth for themselves and help society function better as well?"

(Notice I didn't say these were easy questions. That's why we haven't found all the answers yet!)

What about the problems people face on the personal or professional level?

Wanting to be more successful: "How can I be more successful in my life and business?"

Lack of organization: "Why can't I find what I'm looking for?"

Wanting companionship: "Why can't I meet the person of my dreams?"

If you want to change any of these, you could use the traditional affirmation method by saying things like: *"I am a success, I am organized, I am good enough,"* and so on.

You may believe these statements, and you may not. Now, if affirmations work for you, that's great. If, however, you find yourself not believing your affirmations (like most of us), and you're not totally satisfied with the results, why not try something so simple, yet so powerful, that the traditional success teachers skipped right over it on their way to breakfast:

Rather than making a statement you don't believe . . . why not ask a QUESTION that can transform your life?

HOW YOU CREATE YOUR LIFE

The staggering realization I made in The Shower on that fateful morning in 1997 was that you are creating the reality of your life at this very moment in two ways: by the statements you say to yourself and others, and by *the questions you ask yourself and others*.

Traditional success teachers have focused a great deal of energy telling you to change your statements. But until The Shower, no one had fully realized, or shown how to harness, the awesome power of what happens when you change the *questions*.

Your mind has what you might call an **Automatic Search Function,** which means that when you ask yourself a question, your mind automatically begins to search for an answer. (Psychologists have referred to this function of the human brain as the *embedded presupposition factor.)*

The greatest teachers throughout history have taught the truth of the statement, "As you sow, so shall you reap." This is often called The Law of Sowing and Reaping (Emerson called it First Law) or The Law of Attraction, which means that what you focus on (the thought-seeds you continually plant) will grow and bear fruit.

Traditional teachers told you to change your thinking if you want to change your life. And that's quite correct. What they told you, however, was almost exclusively to change the *statements* you're making—while almost completely ignoring the *questions* you're asking.

Yet even as far back as Biblical times, we've been reminded, "You have not because you ask not," and "Ask and you shall receive."

If you only change the *statements* you say without changing the QUESTIONS you ask, you're missing out on the fastest, easiest way to change your life that's ever been discovered.

HOW A 13-YEAR-OLD GIRL CURED
HER COMPULSIVE WORRYING

I got a call one day from Mary, a professional salesperson from Wisconsin who had attended one of our *Secret Code of Success* workshops. The first words out of her mouth were, "Your work has been life-changing to me!" When I asked her what she meant, she told me the following story:

> After attending your seminar and learning how to use Afformations, I realized that if it could work for me, it could also work for my 13-year-old daughter Stefanie. She's a high achiever who gets all A's in school, but she's also a chronic and compulsive worrier.
>
> Stefanie worried so much that she had severe sleeping problems. She'd lay awake many nights worrying, until finally she'd come into our bedroom and wake us from a sound sleep so we could comfort her.
>
> We tried everything. We read to her. We prayed with her. We were even considering taking her to therapy. Still the worrying—and the sleepless nights—continued. She would cry and ask me, "Why do I worry so much?" It broke my heart because I couldn't help my own daughter.
>
> Finally, when I heard you teach Afformations at your seminar, I realized this could be the answer I'd been praying for! When I came back from your seminar, I taught Stefanie how to use Afformations, and we talked for a long time about what questions would make the most difference in her life.
>
> She was as excited as I was! The questions we came up with were:
>
> *"Why am I worry-free?"*
> *"Why do I enjoy a full night's sleep?"*
> *"Why do I put my trust in God's hands?"*
> *"Why do all my friends love me?"*
> *"Why do I love me?"*

Now she's a different kid!

From the very first day she started using Afformations—it was truly miraculous, like turning on a dime!—Stefanie's worrying stopped. She also became much happier, more relaxed, and seems to be at peace in her own skin. And you know how hard that can be for teenagers nowadays—especially teenage girls!

Your books were first self-help books I've ever read where I actually DID the exercises. Thank you for making such a difference in our lives!

Mary then told me that not only did Afformations improve her own business and enable her daughter to quit worrying, she also started sharing Afformations with everyone she met.

When her husband Scott told her that he wasn't passionate about his work, Mary began afforming, *"Why is the right calling coming to Scott?"* Within weeks, he landed his dream position. And get this: It was a position at Stefanie's high school, exactly where he wanted to be. How's that for manifesting?

EMPOWERING VS. DISEMPOWERING QUESTIONS

Do you know what most people are doing with their lives? Most people are unknowingly asking negative, disempowering questions—and wondering why they're not getting the results they dream of.

Let's examine these empowering vs. disempowering questions. We'll start with *dis*empowering questions, because while they're the kind you may be most familiar with, they're also the ones you want to get rid of as soon as possible.

These are questions like, *"Why am I so afraid? Why doesn't anyone love me? How come I never get the breaks other people get?"* No one asks these questions consciously or on purpose, but you may be asking them without knowing it.

Try this. Consciously ask these disempowering questions out loud. See how you feel when you ask yourself: *"Why don't I have enough money? How come I'm so lonely? Why am I such a loser? Why can't I do anything right?"* Doesn't feel too good, does it?

The ultimate result of asking disempowering questions—whether conscious or not—is that you manifest what you focus on. In other words, when you ask negative questions, you get negative results.

Use the space below to list the five most disempowering questions you hear in your head. Yes, I mean right now.

They may have come from someone in your past, or it could be something you made up on your own. It's vital that you know exactly what your hidden disempowering questions are, so you can begin to consciously turn them around. (Note: You might want to write the date next to your questions, so when you return to this book later, you'll see just how far you've progressed.)

Please do this right now. I'll be right here when you get back.

THE FIVE MOST DISEMPOWERING
QUESTIONS I HEAR IN MY HEAD

1.

2.

3.

4.

5.

Whew. Pretty bad, aren't they?
Are you ready to find a better way?

EMPOWERING QUESTIONS = THE RIGHT QUESTIONS

Now that you've identified what your individual *dis*empowering questions are, you may be asking, "What are *empowering* questions—and how can I start asking them instead of the negative ones?" Glad you asked!

Empowering questions cause your mind to focus on *what you have* vs. *what you lack*. Asking empowering questions leads to feelings of self-esteem and a positive self-image—because your mind automatically begins to focus on what's RIGHT about you, instead of what's wrong with you. Empowering questions, therefore, lead directly to answers that tell the truth about Who You Really Are.

Let's change your disempowering questions from the previous list to empowering questions. How? Simply reverse the negative questions to positive! For example, if your disempowering question is, *"Why am I such a loser?"* your empowering question would be, *"Why am I such a success?"*

All right, grab your pen and get ready to experience the difference . . .

FIVE NEW EMPOWERING QUESTIONS
I'M GOING TO START ASKING

1.

2.

3.

4.

5.

Pretty cool, huh?

Did you notice something shift in your mind?

Guess what? You've just taken the first Step of *The Secret Code of Success.*

The purpose of Afformations is to change your disempowering questions to empowering questions.

By doing this, you will gain conscious control of the thought-seeds you're planting . . .

Which will, through The Law of Attraction, change your life.

HOW AN INSURANCE SALESMAN WENT FROM $1,500 A MONTH TO $120,000 A YEAR

Brandon, an insurance salesman from Utah, called our offices one day and I happened to pick up the phone. I liked him immediately. He was warm, open, and told me that he had spent over $30,000 on every self-help program under the sun—yet he was still only making about $1,500 a month.

Brandon had heard about our programs and decided to invest in the home-study materials we offer. Here's what happened next, in Brandon's own words:

After spending over a decade and more than $30,000 on everything from books, tapes, and seminars to actually becoming certified as an NLP practitioner, what has happened to me as a result of using Afformations is nothing short of amazing.

After going through Noah's home-study materials just once, I realized that I was asking myself disempowering questions that were stopping my growth, like *"Why can't I get any new referrals?"*

I immediately started asking myself positive Afformations.

First, I began asking, *"Why do I get referrals every day?"* Within four days I had received <u>nine new referrals</u> to new clients—that was completely unlike any numbers I had gotten in the past.

And the fun didn't stop there!

I wrote a list of 150 different Afformations that I began carrying around in my pocket.

My favorite? *"Why is it so easy and so okay for me to have, do, and be anything I want?"*

Before I met Noah, my sales averaged between $1,500 and $2,000 a month. In the first month of using Noah's program, my sales <u>tripled</u>. (Remember, these numbers are crunched by an insurance company!)

By the end of the year, my personal income had QUINTU-PLED, and I was named Agent of the Year. This was in spite of going through a divorce and my grandmother passing away.

After that first year, I realized I was ready to get back into a relationship. So I began afforming: *"Why am I so lucky to meet the perfect girl for me so quickly?"*

In less than forty days, I met a fantastic woman—but what's truly miraculous is that if we'd met just one week earlier, I wouldn't have been open to meeting her, because I wanted someone over 21 years old (I was 27 at the time)—and we met just four days after her twenty-first birthday!

My advice? Do this work. It can save you years of your life and many, many thousands of dollars!

WHY ARE THEY CALLED AF*FORM*ATIONS?

Let's return to what we've learned already: The human mind operates by asking and answering questions. Therefore, when you ask yourself a question repeatedly, your mind must search for an answer to your question.

I named this process of using empowering questions the use

of Afformations, or **The Afformation Method.** So where did the word *Afformation* come from?

One thing you should know about me: I was a geek before they put the word *computer* in front of it. In high school, I didn't have shoulder-length hair; I had shoulder-width hair.

As a geek, one of my favorite subjects was Latin. After The Shower, I found that the word *affirmation* comes from the Latin *firmare*, which means "to make firm." I began asking myself, "If affirmations are positive statements, what would the perfect word be to describe empowering questions?"

I realized that when we ask questions of ourselves or others—whether positive or negative—we are really *forming* new thought patterns, which *form* a new life for us.

The word *form* comes from the Latin *formare,* which means "to form or give shape to." And that's when it hit me:

What if you're making something FIRM . . . But it's in the wrong FORM?

That would be called "a life you don't want"!

For example: *"Why am I so broke?"* You *formed* it . . . it becomes *firm* . . . and there's your life!

It was then that I realized the real reason affirmations aren't very effective for changing our lives: because we're trying to make something *firm* before we've *formed* what we really want.

I realized that instead of making something *firm*, we first need to *form* questions that would change the thought-seeds we were sowing, which would change our lives.

And that's how the word—and the teaching of—Afformations was born.

(By the way, it's perfectly legitimate to invent a new word to describe a new way of looking at the universe. For example, a very short time ago in human history, the words *Internet, Google,* even *software* didn't exist. These words had no meaning because the technology they describe didn't exist. Now, of course, we use these terms every day. In this book, I'm describing a new technology of the mind. Hence, Afformations: a new word to describe a new technology.)

THE BOTTOM LINE: YOU'RE ALREADY DOING THIS

In case you're still wondering if this works, or thinking this is the nuttiest thing you've ever heard, let us offer you one final fact:

You are already using Afformations
all the time anyway.

Thoughts like *"Why am I so stupid?"* or *"Why can't I do anything right?"* are simply negative Afformations! These questions are really your head trash forming itself inside your mind, thereby forming your very life.

Once, during one of our *Secret Code of Success* seminars in Virginia, a young couple came up to me, literally jumping up and down with excitement. They said they'd heard me teach Afformations at their company's national sales conference just a few months earlier. Here's their story:

At your seminar, we heard you explain how to use Afformations to change your life. We'd been doing affirmations for the past four years just as we were instructed: We made affirmation tapes, said them to one another, placed them on our refrigerator, even hung affirmation signs in the shower. Well, all we got was a bunch of wet words!

After hearing you speak about Afformations at your workshop, we were very excited. We realized the power of asking ourselves empowering questions and letting our minds search for the answers. We started to use Afformations in exactly the same way we'd been using traditional affirmations: We asked each other our new questions, placed them on our refrigerator, and talked about our new Afformations day after day.

The results were absolutely amazing! We attended your seminar in July. By August, we realized we were doing a lot of things differently because of the Afformations we learned from you. And in September, we qualified for our first Cadillac! After more than *four years* of using traditional affirmations with little to show for it, we got the exact results we wanted *in less than ninety days using Afformations.*

This professional couple had been very committed to using the traditional method. They'd even said affirmations out loud to one another—now that's commitment! Yet affirmations simply didn't enable them to overcome their subconscious negative beliefs.

Using Afformations, their minds began to search for new, creative ways to find solutions to their problems. And the results spoke for themselves.

The power to create your life using Afformations lies within you and your miraculous, marvelous mind. Since you're already using them anyway, why not use them *consciously* to create the life you want . . . rather than unconsciously creating a life you don't?

THE FOUR STEPS TO CREATE AFFORMATIONS THAT CAN CHANGE YOUR LIFE

Step 1: Ask yourself what you want.

You've probably done this Step before. In Step 1, you can use goals you've previously written, or start from scratch. You decide. The point is to determine what it is that you want.

(Please note that traditional success literature stops right here! They told us to "set your goals," and then say affirmations that attempt to convince your brain that you will have what you want . . . sometime.)

For example, in Step 1, you might decide that your goal is to be happy, healthy, and wealthy (hard to imagine anyone not wanting those things). So, you would write: *"I want to be happy, healthy, and wealthy."*

Now we go to the breakthrough Step . . .

Step 2: Form a question that assumes that *What You Want is already true*.

In Step 2, you ask a question that *assumes* that what you want is already so, has already happened, or is already true.

This is the key step to creating Afformations that can change your life.

In the example above, what you want is to be happy, healthy, and wealthy, right? Well, in this Step you ask yourself why this is already so!

Your life is a reflection of the thought-seeds you plant and give energy to. More precisely, your life is a reflection of the *unconscious assumptions* you make about life and your relationship to it.

For example, if you grew up in an environment where there wasn't a lot of money, and your family made you aware that the lack of money was the cause of their unhappiness, you might conclude that there's a lack of money in the world that leads to unhappiness, and that's just the way life is.

If you could find a mechanism that could record your subconscious thought-seeds and play them back to you, they might sound something like this: *"Why am I so broke? Why don't I have enough? Why aren't I more successful?"* and so forth.

Well, a mechanism does exist that records and reflects your subconscious thought-seeds—that mechanism is called Your Life!

THIS IS YOUR LIFE

So here you are, asking yourself these unconscious negative questions. What do you think the answers to these negative questions would be? The answers would be: *Your life showing up as the results of the negative questions you've been asking—the natural fruits of negative thought-seeds.* For example:

If you've been unconsciously asking, *"Why am I so unhappy?"* you'll get the answer as your unhappy life.

If you've been unknowingly asking, *"Why don't I have enough?"* the answer will appear as your lack in life.

If you've been unwittingly asking, *"Why am I so lonely?"* the person of your dreams will keep not showing up.

REVERSE THE CURSE

When you do this Step of The Afformation Method, you will take what has been subconscious (hidden) and make it conscious (visible), and take what is negative (disempowering) and make it positive (empowering).

Let's reverse all the negative questions shown above. The reverse might look something like this:

Why am I so happy?
Why do I have enough?
Why am I so loved?

These questions may seem unfamiliar, even crazy, to you right now. But what if you allowed yourself to accept those questions as *the truth about your life?*

Wouldn't you have a life that's different than the average person's—*a life that's different from the one you have now?*

**The quality of your life depends on just two things:
the quality of your communication with
the world *inside* yourself, and the quality of
your communication with the world *outside* yourself.**

Step 2 of The Afformations Method is to begin to change the quality of communication with the world *inside* yourself. You will begin to ask yourself new, better, *em*powering questions, and stop asking yourself negative, *dis*empowering questions.

This is the fastest, most effective way I've ever seen to immediately change the quality of your communication with both your inside and outside worlds.

So Step 2 in The Afformation Method is to ask yourself, *"Why is [what I want] true in my life now?"*

Using our example above, you would ask yourself, *"Why am I so happy, healthy, and wealthy?"*

Step 3: Give yourself to the question.

The point of Afformations does not lie in finding the answer, but in *asking better questions*. When you ask better questions, your mind will automatically focus on things you've probably never focused on before. When you do this, the results will amaze you.

I got the following letter from my friend John Adams of The Golden Key Ministry in Phoenix . . .

Dear Noah,

I want to tell you a true story about my friends Sam and Shirley, two people I had taught The Afformations Method to about three years ago when I first read your Afformations book.

Shirley had been accepted into the ministerial program at Unity in Missouri, so they planned to sell their home and move to Kansas City. They put their home on the market in early April with no results. People would come and look but no one was buying.

On Saturday, May 5, Sam and Shirley told me about their lack of a buyer for their home.

Because they needed to leave in early June, they were getting nervous and wanted my advice.

I suggested they go through every room in their home, bless it, and begin afforming, "Why is this house now easily sold to the right party for the right price?"

That was Saturday. The next afternoon, a couple came and looked at the house. On Tuesday, they made an offer, which was too low. Sam & Shirley kept their Afformation going and made a higher, counter offer which was accepted on Tuesday afternoon!

Everything went through quickly and the deal closed on May 31st. Sam & Shirley are on their way to Missouri as true believers!

Let's say you want to find a new restaurant in your city. You go to Google and type the key word *restaurants* and the city you're in. What you're really doing is *asking a question you don't know the answer to, yet.*

When you Google something, do you sit there and worry that Google won't be able to answer your question? No, you just hit Enter and know the answer's on its way. When you type in a question, can Google say, "I don't feel like answering your question right now"? No, it just searches for the answer; and you *trust* that not only is the answer out there, it's now on its way to you.

It's the same with Afformations. You do not need to know, for example, why you are rich. You do, however, need to ask *why you are rich.* Why? Because asking that kind of empowering question automatically focuses your mind on *what you have* vs. *what you lack.*

Most people are coming from lack. *Coming from lack* means your mind is focused on what you don't have. When you're focused on what you don't have, what do you get more of? Feelings of not having!

And where does that focus come from? From the questions you're unconsciously asking. Your mind operates like Google, only on a much more powerful level. That's because Google can't change its questions; it can only do what it's asked. You, however, can consciously *choose* your questions.

Once you ask a question of your mind, whether or not you know it, your mind automatically starts to search for the answer without your conscious volition.

Which brings us to the fourth essential Step of The Afformations Method—the final one you must do if you want this method to work for you . . .

Step 4: Take new ACTIONS based on your new assumptions about life.

You are, right now, making hundreds, perhaps thousands of unconscious assumptions about life and your relationship to it. These assumptions form the basis of how you go through life—positively or negatively, with confidence or shyness, from *lack* or from *enough*, from love or from fear.

For instance, if you assume that life is *for* you, you will naturally take actions based on the belief that "things will work out for the best"—and your results will naturally follow. If you assume that life is *against* you, however, then your actions will be hesitant, based on fear and "why bother"—and your results will naturally follow.

The Afformations Method makes conscious and clear that which has, until now, been subconscious and hidden.

For example, a confident person will have an easier time in life, whether building relationships or building a business. Traditional teachers told us that we should be confident. But where does the behavior of *confidence* really come from? It comes from your hidden, subconscious assumptions about how life is going to treat you.

You are continually forming assumptions about life and your

relationship to it; but these assumptions are nearly always subconscious—so hidden, you don't even realize they're there.

As a result, the great percentage of your actions are governed by assumptions you may have formed years—even decades—ago!

If you grew up with the assumption that life is lack, what would your actions be? How confident would you be about building your business or meeting new people?

Remember, the point of The Afformation Method is not to find "the answer" to your questions. The point is to change *what your mind automatically focuses on*. Since you are now going to form *positive* questions that assume that *what you want* is already true, your mind has no choice but to find a way to make it so.

Can you see how this process must, by definition, change your life?

HOW YOU'LL KNOW WHEN IT'S WORKING

One question I hear a lot about Afformations is: "How will I know when it's working?" (This question, by the way, typically comes from people who haven't tried it, consciously, yet.) Many people who start using Afformations report an almost instant feeling of calm and peace of mind.

However, the Afformations Method is based on science, not magic. You cannot ask yourself, *"Why am I so thin and healthy?"* while continuing to eat unhealthy foods, and expect to lose weight. You cannot break the laws of the universe by sowing positive questions and continuing to do negative or self-defeating behaviors, and expect to get what you want.

The point of Afformations is not to try and trick your mind, but to use it properly. You're already using this method anyway, but most people are using it unconsciously, in a negative or self-defeating way.

Use Afformations, but don't worry about doing them "right." There's more going on in the Subconscious Mind than science will probably ever figure out. But using Afformations will enable your mind's Automatic Search Function to produce remarkable results in your favor, rather than negative ones you don't want.

HOW TO USE THE REST OF THIS BOOK

The rest of this book includes the top ten most powerful Afformations I've used and taught my Students for the seven Steps of *The Secret Code of Success*. Naturally, since the number of Afformations you can create is literally infinite, don't feel confined by these ten.

We've left room for you to write your own Afformations that suit your individual situation. You can also refer to my other books in The Afformation Series. (See *Additional Resources* at the back of the book, come to one of our *Secret Code of Success* seminars, or visit **SecretCodeBook.com**.)

Use them, go over them again and again, and write them out as you would your traditional affirmations—but notice that Afformations may flow much more easily for you!

That's because rather than trying to force yourself to believe something that you don't really believe, you'll be forming new assumptions about life and your relationship to it, based on what you really do want.

I know of no other method that can yield such dramatic results with so little effort. Using Afformations, you can take direct, conscious control of your subconscious thoughts—change the questions, change your results, and change your life!

For more information on how to use Afformations to get what you want twice as fast with half the effort, visit **www.Afformations.com**.

A QUICK RECAP

1. The human mind works using questions. Human thought is really *the process of asking and searching for the answers to questions.*

2. Traditional success teachers have told us for decades to use affirmations or positive statements to get what we wanted. The problem is, affirmations don't really work because you're trying to convince yourself of something you don't believe.

3. The author discovered Afformations, which are empowering *questions* (not statements) that immediately change your subconscious thought patterns from negative to positive. Because your mind automatically starts to search for the answers to questions, asking empowering questions immediately changes your focus from what you don't have to what you have.

4. The four Steps of The Afformations Method are:

1. Ask yourself what you want.
2. Form a question that assumes that what you want is already true.
3. Let your mind search for the answer.
4. Take new ACTIONS based on your new assumptions about life.

5. You can use Afformations in any aspect of your life: money, health, relationships, weight loss, sales, etc. Use Afformations and you can begin to manifest what you want, twice as fast with half the effort.

Next Actions: List three things you can do from this chapter in the next seven days to use Afformations for faster, better results in your life, career, and relationships.

1. _____

2. _____

3. _____

TOP 10 AFFORMATIONS FOR STEP 1:

1. Why am I so rich?

2. Why am I so happy?

3. Why am I enough?

4. Why am I good enough?

5. Why do I have what it takes to succeed?

6. Why do I have the courage to do what I love?

7. Why does opportunity come to me so easily now?

8. Why do I enjoy so much success?

9. Why do I have more than enough money in my business?

10. Why does having what I want help others get what they want?

CHAPTER 5

Step 2: Loving Mirrors and Safe Havens

**Relationship is a mirror in which you can see yourself,
not as you would wish to be, but as you are.**

—JIDDU KRISHNAMURTI

I want you to think for a moment about your eyes. What color are they?

I'll bet you know what color your eyes arc. But, how do you know? How did you determine your own eye color? The answer is, you either looked in a mirror (or another reflective substance like a photograph), or someone told you. In fact, those are the only two ways to determine your own eye color.

Right now, I want you to see your own eye color without looking in a mirror. Come on . . . *Get motivated, work hard, set your goals!*

I don't care how smart, cute, talented, or motivated you are; you simply cannot see your own eye color by looking from within yourself. While it may seem improbable, that simple analogy forms the foundation of this entire System.

GEORGE AND CLARENCE

Remember the movie *It's a Wonderful Life*? In that movie, Jimmy Stewart played George Bailey, a wonderful guy who helped many people, yet had a really bad case of low self-esteem. He had decided to commit suicide because he literally believed he was more valuable dead than alive (remember that insurance policy?). Then Clarence, his guardian angel, came down from heaven and showed him what life would have been like if George had never been born.

That's when George understood for the first time that his life had value and meaning. That's why his paradigm shifted and he realized that his was, in fact, a wonderful life.

Now, what do you think would have happened if George Bailey had looked in a mirror and said to himself, "I'm good enough, I'm smart enough, and gosh darn it, people like me"? What if he had simply thought positive and tried to psych himself up?

What if he had *set his goals* and said, "I'm gonna get motivated now"? What if he had used visualization techniques, or affirmations, or vision boards? Do you really think that would have created such a powerful transformation in his life? Me neither.

What I have just shown you is one of the great and sad ironies of traditional success programs, because they've tried to get us motivated by telling us to "set our goals" and that we should believe in ourselves.

Let me ask you a question. When you set your goals, whom are you going to? You are going to yourself.

Yet, who is the worst person to know what you are truly capable of? You!

Aren't we often the worst judge of what we're really capable of doing? Aren't we sometimes our own worst enemy? Well, if what you want is love, support, and encouragement, is it really smart to go to your worst enemy?

**You are the *least* capable person to know
what you're truly capable *of.***

What I'm showing you is the complete *opposite* of what they taught us in traditional success programs. Going back to your eyes example: No matter how hard you work, how long you try, or how motivated you are, you can never see your own eyes by looking from within yourself. Yet your eyes are an essential part of you! They are your windows to the world and the windows to your very soul. Yet, you can never see them without the help of someone or something outside of you.

WHAT CAUSES YOUR HEAD TRASH

Let's take this analogy one step further. Let's say you have brown eyes; but everyone around you, even the people closest to you, have told you since the beginning of your life that you have blue eyes. And let's say that you had no other way to corroborate that information. What would you be forced to believe about yourself?

Because of the information you've been given, plus the fact that you can't see your own eyes directly, you would be forced to believe that you have blue eyes; but that's completely false information about you.

Have you ever been in a funhouse? What do funhouses have— funhouse mirrors, right? And what does a funhouse mirror do? It distorts you. You're looking at it, and it's kind of weird. It looks sort of like you, but it's not you. It's an *inaccurate representation* of you.

But what if a funhouse mirror was the only mirror you had ever looked in? What if that distorted reflection was the only one from which you'd received information about you? What then would you be forced to believe about yourself?

| NEGATIVE REFLECTION | AUTHENTIC SELF | LOVING MIRROR |

You would be forced to believe that the distorted image was what you really looked like. You would have no choice but to believe the inaccurate image because it's the only one you've ever seen.

So let me ask you something: Were you raised in a funhouse? Are you still in the funhouse? Have you ever seen yourself accurately reflected by those around you?

Sadly, most of us have never seen ourselves accurately reflected by those around us, even (especially) those closest to us. A funhouse mirror distorts your *physical* image. In the same way, when we receive inaccurate information about Who We Are, our **Authentic Self** is distorted. When Who We Are is not accurately reflected by those around us, we develop what I call a **Negative Reflection**.

Your Negative Reflection represents the head trash that most of us are carrying around. It's that little voice that says, "You can't do it. Who do you think you are? No one in our family does that!"

While your Authentic Self knows you're good enough, your Negative Reflection tells you, "You're not good enough. I could never do that. Maybe 'they' could do it, but I'll never be able to." Sound familiar?

We all have our own unique head trash, our own Negative Reflection. But amazingly, that's not the real problem.

WHY YOU DON'T BELIEVE IN YOURSELF (YET)

Traditional success teachers told us, "Well, if you have negative thoughts, just think positive. Believe in yourself. Set your goals." Do you think that would have worked for George Bailey? Do you honestly think he would've been able to "set his goals" and get out of his miserable situation with this kind of advice?

Yes, I know it was just a movie. But what about YOUR life? How many times have you tried this? How many times have you tried to psych yourself up and do what they told you to do—think positive, believe in yourself, set your goals? How has that been working for you?

You can keep trying to put a nail in the wall with the chainsaw they gave you . . . or you can pick up a hammer. I'm giving you the hammer, and it's called *the support of people who believe in you, more than you believe in yourself.*

This is one of the greatest ironies of this work—because the Three Percenters have been telling us for decades, "Believe in yourself." But they don't realize that what they're saying is completely backwards.

It's not that believing in yourself is wrong, any more than a chainsaw is wrong. It's just that when they tell you to believe in yourself, they have the order wrong. That's because believing in yourself is the last, not the first, stage in the evolution of Success.

The first stage is *someone believes in you.*

The second stage is *you believe in someone else.*

The final stage is *you believe in you.*

WHY THIS FLIPS TRADITIONAL SUCCESS LITERATURE ON ITS HEAD

In traditional success programs, what's the first thing they told us to do? Exactly: *Set your goals.*

Who are you going to, to set your goals? You.

But who is the worst person to know what you're really capable of? *You.*

In traditional success programs, they implicitly told you to go to yourself to set your goals, because that's what the Three Percenters did. They believed in themselves, so they naturally assumed that you and I did, too.

But here's the problem. When I asked them exactly how they came to believe in themselves, every multi-millionaire I've ever coached or become friends with has finally told me that they would not have achieved their level of success without the loving support and encouragement of *someone who believed in them when they didn't even believe in themselves.*

Just like George Bailey had Clarence the Angel, these Three Percenters each had someone who was their guardian angel here on Earth. But they hadn't realized how essential that was until I asked them!

You can corroborate what I'm saying from your own life experience. Think back to when someone saw something greater in you than you ever saw in yourself. Remember that time when someone looked at you and saw that greatness in you, that spark, that *something* in you that you never would have seen in yourself. Remember that?

Maybe it was a coach, a teacher, or a mentor. Maybe it was a parent, spouse, or friend. Maybe it was your grandma, grandpa, uncle, aunt, or somebody close to you. Whoever it was, they saw something in you, encouraged you and said, "I know you can do this. I see wonderful things in you. I see the leader in you. And I know you can do it."

And you're standing there going, "Who, me?"

You have that response because you can't fully perceive your own value, any more than you can see your own eyes. We don't fully comprehend our own value to the world. I call this phenomenon **The Loving Mirror Principle**, and it's the hidden aspect of Success that almost everyone ignores.

WHAT IS A LOVING MIRROR?

A **Loving Mirror** is a person who gives you *unconditional support*. Why is this the foundational step to getting rid of your head trash for good?

Just like you can never see your own eyes by looking from within yourself, you can never fully understand your true value from within yourself. It takes the loving support and encouragement from someone like a friend, teacher, coach, or mentor to show you what you are truly capable of.

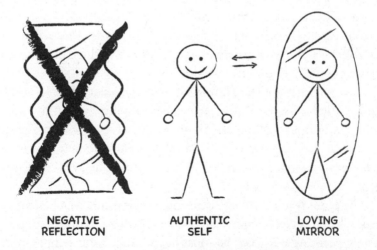

NEGATIVE   AUTHENTIC   LOVING
REFLECTION   SELF   MIRROR

There's a scene from the movie *Facing the Giants* that has become very popular online, because people have passed it from friend to friend hundreds of thousands of times. In the scene, the football coach pushes Brock, the team captain, further than Brock would have ever pushed himself. The coach asks Brock to crawl on his hands and feet—without putting his knees down!—across a football field with one of his teammates on his back. But then the coach did something monumentally clever: he blindfolded Brock. Why? Because he didn't want Brock to give up before he gave it his "very best."

Brock thought he could only make it to the 30-yard line; but with the coach's encouragement—okay, yelling—Brock did "The Death Crawl" the entire length of a football field. This movie shows one of the most powerful and moving examples of the Loving Mirror Principle in action. Maybe that's why so many people have passed it along to their friends. (To see "The Death Crawl" scene in its entirety, visit **www.SecretCodeBook.com/deathcrawl.**)

GAINING UNCONDITIONAL SUPPORT FOR YOUR LIFE

Human beings perform best in an environment of unconditional support. That happens when someone looks at you and sees your full capacity, potential, and greatness. That person *knows* that you can do it, *sees* that you can do it, and *holds* you to that. They are the ones who say, "I know you can do this."

Have you ever noticed that we can see positive qualities in others, but usually have a hard time seeing them in ourselves? Many of us were taught not to think too highly of ourselves, not to brag, and not to get "too big for our britches." (What I want to know is: Who wears britches any more, anyway—and why are they always so small?)

The point is, many of us are afraid of being called "arrogant" or "stuck on ourselves"—and that's not at all what I'm suggesting. I'm merely pointing out that the most happy, successful people in the world became that way because someone believed in them, usually more than they believed in themselves.

You might say, "But Noah, I don't have anyone who believes in me!" That's the #1 objection I hear when I present this Step at my seminars. You need to realize: *That's the very point.* If you weren't lucky enough to have been born into a family of Loving Mirrors (as most of us weren't), you can now find them as an adult.

SAFE HAVENS: THE LOVING MIRROR AT WORK

Okay, I can hear what you're saying. "Noah, I can see how this principle works in my personal life. But I bought this book so I could learn how to make more money! Now you're telling me all this touchy-feely stuff? What about work, business, my career? It's a dog-eat-dog world out there. How does this principle apply to the everyday demands of my business?"

That's the second-most common objection I hear in my seminars. Now, last time I checked, you have to *do something* in order to get the thing called money. Generally speaking, you can't walk into a room and say, "Okay, everybody, love me and give me lots of money." If that's your job, I want your job! The way it typically works on the planet Earth is: First, you provide value to other human beings, and only then do they give you the thing called money.

Because you have to *do something* in order to get the thing called money, it's clear that work is *conditional*. Yet, we've already seen that human beings perform best when they're supported *unconditionally*—when someone believes in you more than you believe in yourself.

How, then, do we solve the Conditional/Unconditional Dichotomy?

We solve it with what I call the **Safe Haven**. A Safe Haven is someone who sees your capacity and potential, someone who holds you to a higher standard and keeps you accountable to the demands of business. In other words, the Safe Haven doesn't let you get away with NOT living up to what you're really capable of.

YOUR PERSONAL TRAINER

A great example of this is a personal trainer. If you've ever worked with a personal trainer, you know she's basically a drill sergeant (hopefully, an encouraging one, but a drill sergeant nonetheless). She'll say things like, "You can do this, and you've got to do it. Let's go!"

Left to our own devices, what do we do when we work out? We go, "Time for sit-ups. Ready? One, two . . . okay, I'm good."

But a good personal trainer would never let you get away with that. You're there working and sweating, saying, "I can't do it," but she's there going, "Yes, you can!"

You: "No, I can't!"

Her: "Yes, you can!"

You: "No, I can't!"

Her: "Yes, you can!"

You: (pause) "Hey, I did it."

Your trainer pushes and pushes you because she knows you can do it. She has confidence in you, and gets that performance out of you that you didn't believe you could do.

That's the Safe Haven. You're saying you can't; they're saying, "Yes, you can." A Safe Haven gives you the unconditional support you need, and holds you to a higher standard than you would ever hold yourself to. And he does it because he believes in you, even when you may not believe in yourself.

Loving Mirrors and Safe Havens form the core of *The Secret Code of Success,* for the very reason that you can't see your own value. If you don't do this Step, there's no reason for you to do anything else. Why? Because every Three Percenter had at least one Loving Mirror show them their value at one point in their lives. And that, without their conscious awareness, is precisely what gave them permission to succeed.

Bottom line: If you want to be happy and rich, you must find Loving Mirrors for your life and Safe Havens for your business. There is no way around this.

THEY CALLED HIM BUTTERFINGERS

There was once a pro football wide receiver nicknamed Butterfingers because, even though he was a first-round draft pick out of college, in his first pro season, he couldn't catch the ball. A super-talented kid from a small town in Mississippi, his coaches and fellow players saw his raw ability, but because his team was based in San Francisco, he was thousands of miles from friends and family. He was lonely and to top it all off, he felt he was letting his teammates down.

So he went to his coach and told him he was going to quit. His coach, a very smart man named Bill Walsh, said this to him:

"Son, I'm not going to let you quit. I've seen what you can do out there. God has gifted you with the ability to play this game. I know you're a long way from home, but your teammates believe in you. I believe in you. I know you can do it, and I'm not going to let you quit, because I think you're going to be one of the greatest receivers this game has ever seen."

After Bill Walsh said this to him, the light went on. This young man became the hardest-working man in the NFL. His workouts became the stuff of legend. He would run drill after drill after drill, the first one on the field in the morning and the last one to leave. They would have to turn the stadium lights out on him!

And by the end of his first season, Jerry Rice was on his way to becoming the greatest wide receiver in the history of the game. He owns every NFL record for wide receivers, including most career receptions (1,549), yards receiving (22,895—that's over 13 MILES!), and touchdowns receiving (197).

All this happened because one man, Bill Walsh, believed in him when Jerry Rice couldn't even believe in himself. So if you think what I'm teaching here sounds touchy-feely, let me assure you: This principle is the most powerful, results-creating, bottom-line-focused method to get your foot off the brake that's ever been identified. It's also the hidden principle that every happy, successful person, team, or organization has used—whether or not they know it.

GAINING UNCONDITIONAL SUPPORT
FOR YOUR BUSINESS

Not one of my multi-millionaire friends has ever told me, "Oh, yeah, I did it all by myself. I didn't need anybody." If you insist on being the lone wolf—and many of my Students did when they first came to me (that's precisely why they were struggling)—then my work with countless thousands of students shows that you are going to struggle for a long, long time.

Trying to succeed without the support of others is like standing on a gold mine, digging away with a teaspoon.

Many people right now are standing on a gold mine, digging away with their teaspoons called "don't ask for help" or "I don't have anyone"—while right under their noses stands a brand-new, never-used backhoe called their Loving Mirrors and Safe Havens.

That gold, that treasure, lies inside you . . . so let's start uncovering it together.

GET RID OF THE BULLY IN YOUR HEAD

Here's the first exercise you need to do to get rid of your head trash and get your foot off the brake. You didn't think you were going to get away with just *reading*, did you? Remember, this is a course of ACTION. I mean that in two ways: this System requires that you take ACTION; and, I hate to break this to you, but if you don't do something different from what you've done before, chances are you won't get different results that what you've had in the past.

This exercise is called *"Excavating and Evicting Your Negative Reflection."* Your Negative Reflection—that funhouse mirror you've been looking in—causes your head trash and says things like, "You're not good enough." So the first thing we need to do to get your foot off the brake is to *excavate* your Negative Reflection—get it out in the open—and then *evict* it—tell it to take a hike.

Take out a sheet of paper and draw two columns: one for your Negative Reflection and one for your Authentic Self. First, I want you to write what your Negative Reflection is saying to you. What is your head trash telling you?

Maybe it says, "You can't do it. You'll never make it. You're a fraud. You're a phony, and nobody likes you." Whatever it is, just write it down.

Take as much paper as you want. Don't feel restricted by a sheet of paper. I also suggest that you start a *Secret Code of Success Journal.* Take as long as you want. You don't have to share what you write with anyone else.

In case you're wondering if writing down this negative stuff will give it more power, here are the facts: your Negative Reflection is already in your head. You're simply turning on the light by doing this exercise. The elephant's in the room; ignoring it or pretending it's not there won't make it go away. After all, you've tried that for years, haven't you?

So, get it out in the open, once and for all. Turn the light on, so it won't be hidden anymore—and then we can get rid of it.

EXERCISE: EXCAVATING AND EVICTING YOUR NEGATIVE REFLECTION (THE LIST)

My Negative Reflection What my head trash tells me	My Authentic Self Who I Really Am

Once you've done that, take a deep breath. I know that was not fun. Maybe get up and walk around a bit.

Okay, after you've done that, I want you to get quiet and listen. Just listen to Who You Really Are. Now, write a statement from your Authentic Self.

Your Authentic Self is Who You Really Are, not the bully in your head. That Negative Reflection is just a bully who's been living in your head. Your Authentic Self is that still, small voice within. It's that voice that says, "Hey, you know what: I am good enough. So what if I didn't go to college? A lot of very successful people either didn't go to or didn't finish college. What makes them any better than me? People don't care about that anyway. All they care about is the value that I'm bringing to them."

Or maybe your Authentic Self says, "I am good enough because I am a valuable person and I've had enough of putting myself last. I'm bringing value into people's lives, and I enjoy doing that. I can succeed at whatever I choose and put the work into."

Here are some examples from my Students:

Patty

Negative Reflection	Authentic Self
That I am not smart enough to be successful.	I am in the top 2 percent of intelligent people in this world (how many times do I have to be hit in the head to get this?), and if anyone is smart enough to be successful, it is me.

That my ADD keeps me from being able to focus, and therefore being able to attain success.	I have proven through previous work that I have the ability to be focused and remain on task for long periods of time.

Clare

Negative Reflection	**Authentic Self**
Not sexy	God was nice to me
Too fat	Attractive

Piper

- My negative reflections tell me that I'm not competent, not good enough, that I intimidate & offend others, & that I'm not perceived as authentic.
- My Loving Mirror and Safe Haven are my wonderful husband & my National Sales Director.
- They have helped me see that my true Authentic Self is one of Excellence, Encourager, non-stop enthusiasm that allows for bringing out the best in others. I'm determined, creative, & nurturing.

Write whatever your Authentic Self is saying to you. But you need to get quiet. That's why they call it a *still, small voice*. The Negative Reflection is loud and obnoxious, right in your face. That's what a bully is.

EXERCISE: GET OUT OF THE DARKNESS

After you've written your list, answer these questions:

1. *Who* could I share my list with?

2. *When* can I share it with them?

3. *How* will sharing my list help me gain correct perspective?

4. *What* are specific examples where the Negative Reflection is wrong?

5. *Where* did my Negative Reflection come from?

6. *Why* is that NOT Who I Really Am?

Did you notice something about those questions? They all start with one of Rudyard Kipling's Six Serving Men:

> *I keep six honest serving-men*
> *(They taught me all I knew);*
> *Their names are What and Why and When*
> *And How and Where and Who.*

Questions that begin with these Six Serving Men are designed to elicit *facts*—because Negative Reflection not only lives in secret, it also exists on lies. If you don't gather accurate facts about Who

You Really Are (like if your eyes are brown and not blue), your Negative Reflection will remain strong—by telling lies that you believe.

Share your list with at least one other trusted person. Tell them honestly, "I value you, and I value your opinion. Could you take a look at this?" and ask them to read it and tell you the truth from their perspective.

My Students who've done this have found that the people they share their lists with say to them, "What?! That negative opinion is nothing like you! Where did you get that from?" Many have reported that this exercise was the turning point in their adult lives.

You need to begin seeing yourself through the eyes of your Loving Mirrors, not your Negative Reflection—because, just like you must look in a mirror to see your own eyes, this is the only way to see a correct reflection of you.

When you answer the question, "How will sharing my list help me gain correct perspective?" write your Why-To's (Benefits) of sharing your list with a trusted friend.

Finally, write specific examples where your Negative Reflection is wrong. That's the only other way to kill the Negative Reflection: with facts and data.

For example, my Negative Reflection might say, "Nobody likes having you around." But I could realize, "Wait a minute. Plenty of people like me. I just got off the phone with five different people who really enjoyed talking with me!" So when that Negative Reflection comes back, you simply combat it with the truth.

WHAT'S YOUR SIGN?

Each of us comes into this world as a bright light, good enough.

However, what happens for most of us is that we get negative signs placed on us: *Not good enough. Lazy. Fat. Ugly. Stupid. Everybody would be happier if I weren't around.*

These negative signs are placed on us throughout our lives. They may have been put on us by teachers, peers, family, friends, co-workers, and even ourselves.

When we have signs placed on us, what happens to our light? The light slowly gets covered up. Eventually, it's hard to see—but ironically, the light itself hasn't changed, just the outer visibility of it has dimmed. Nothing about the light inside changed; even these negative signs can't make the light go away.

As far back as Biblical times, humans have been reminded to "Not hide your light under a bushel." What does that tell you? That human beings have been doing this since . . . well, forever. That's why this phenomenon is so common.

If you are old enough to read this book, you're old enough to take responsibility for your life. It's not about pointing fingers and saying, "They did it to me!" No, we're doing the complete opposite—because no successful person is a victim.

Right now, write down the signs that were placed on you. This is the first step to taking responsibility—when you can say, "Yes, these signs may have been placed on me. But I'm taking them off right now, because they're not true."

EXERCISE: THE LAMPPOST AND THE SIGNS

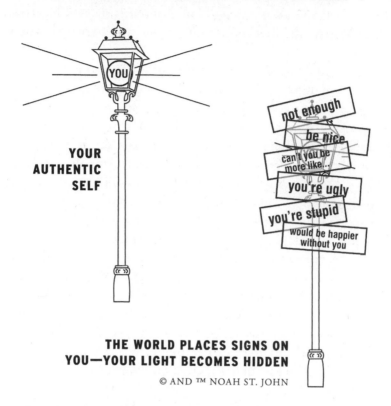

**YOUR
AUTHENTIC
SELF**

not enough
be nice
can't you be
more like...
you're ugly
you're stupid
would be happier
without you

**THE WORLD PLACES SIGNS ON
YOU—YOUR LIGHT BECOMES HIDDEN**

© AND ™ NOAH ST. JOHN

1. What were the top five negative signs placed upon me?

2. What is the reverse of those signs?

3. Who I Really Am/My Authentic Self is:

4. Who will I share this information with?

5. When will I share it with them?

Your negative signs could be something like: *I'm no good; I'm lazy; you're dumb; you're stupid.* (Note that sometimes the Negative Reflection expresses itself as talking to "you" and sometimes refers to "I.")

Now we're going to reverse those signs. For example, the opposite of "I'm dumb" is "I'm smart." The opposite of "I'm not good enough" is "I am good enough." The opposite of "I didn't go to college" is "Who cares?" (People really don't care how about your degree; they care about the degree to which you can help them.)

Next, write your response to, "Who I Really Am/My Authentic Self is . . ." Write a brief statement about your Authentic Self; such as good enough, a child of God, or whatever you want to say. I want you to write something that you can have in the front of your mind, just a quick phrase that's easy to remember.

The last questions are about who you will share this information with and when. Give yourself a deadline, because we want your Negative Reflection out of the darkness—and the only way to do that is to share it with someone else. The Negative Reflection is like a bully in your head. A bully only remains strong when you don't confront it or try to run away from it. When you face it head-on and say, "You talkin' to ME?!" that's when you can be free from the bully in your head.

THE SEVEN KEY SUPPORT QUESTIONS

The next step to identify your Loving Mirrors in your life and Safe Havens for your business is to ask yourself The Seven Key Support Questions:

1. What does *unconditional support* mean to me?
2. What support do I need most in my life right now? In my business?
3. Who would I like to give me that support?

4. What's in it for them to support me? (List Benefits per individual)
5. What would I like to hear from the key people in my life?
6. If there were just one thing I'd ask of them, what would it be?
7. What ACTIONS am I willing to take, to get the support I need?

Key Support Question 1—What does unconditional support mean to me?

I can't tell you what unconditional support means to you. You probably don't know what it means to you. Why? Because you've probably never asked yourself about this. I bet that you didn't realize that it's not only vitally important for your Success, but it's *the most essential Step* to get your foot off the brake.

You can't get around this, and none of the Three Percenters did, either. They either created it unconsciously or always had it. If you've always had something, you don't know what it's like to live without it. But the people who are struggling either do not have this, or don't know how important it is for the success of their lives and businesses.

Key Support Questions 2 & 3—What support do I need most in my life and business? Who would I like to give me that support?

The answers to these two questions may be very similar. For example, if you own your own business, the support you'll need for your life and business are closely related. However, I want you to think about the difference in the support you need for your life, apart from your business. I'm assuming you have a life that is separate from your business. If you don't, we'll fix that in Step 4.

For example, in your life, you might need your spouse to help with the housework, or you might decide you need a housekeeper. In contrast, in your business, maybe you need an executive assistant or a director of marketing. Maybe you need help with a piece of equipment, or maybe you need your upline to work with you more. Use your *Secret Code of Success Journal* and write as much as you want.

Key Support Question 4—What's in it for <u>them</u> to support <u>me</u>?

All human behavior is built on two things—Why-To's and Why-Not-To's. Pros and cons, Costs and Benefits—these are all Why-To's and Why-Not-To's. Nobody does anything that they don't perceive will benefit them. So if you want to get somebody to do something for you, you'd better find out how it's going to benefit them.

For example, I often conduct teleseminars where I promote other authors' programs. Why would I do this? The other author benefits by getting free publicity, plus my web team does all the work. I benefit because more people hear about me and it promotes goodwill among my colleagues. How's that for Why-To's?

Now, I could have approached other authors and said, "Hey, do this because I want more people to hear about me." Do you think anybody would have said, "Gee, where do I sign?" No, I'm pretty sure they would have replied, "Who the heck cares about you?"

That's why I made it ridiculously beneficial to *them*, so they'd have to be crazy not to do it. Free publicity for them, and they don't do any work. Now you're talking.

It's the same thing when you're asking for support. What could be the benefit to *them*? Direct selling or network marketing is the clearest example of this. Do you think your upline will benefit from supporting you? When you start to succeed, what happens to them? Their bank account gets bigger, that's what!

When you get your foot off the brake, everyone above you starts to win more. Gee, I wonder if your upline wants you to succeed more?

Think about this carefully, because when you stop talking about the benefit to you and start communicating the benefits to them, that's when you start to gain the leverage you need to succeed.

The bottom line of human behavior:

Things get very easy when you're always talking about how the other person benefits.

Key Support Question 5—What I'd like to hear from the key people in my life . . .

Most people are starving for attention, appreciation, and recognition. So what would you like to hear? Maybe it's something like "I'm proud of you. You did a great job on that. I love you. I enjoy having you around. I'm just glad you're here." What do you want to hear?

Key Support Question 6—If there were just one thing I'd ask of the key people in my life, it would be . . .

I don't know what it is for you, and you may not know yet. I want you to think about what it would feel like if you could ask just one thing from the key people in your life. "If there were just one thing I'd ask of them, it would be . . ." What?

You may have different people and different situations that you think of. What is the one thing that you would like to ask of these people? If you don't know what that is, it's highly unlikely you'll get the support you want and need. You must be clear. So think about it and write it down.

Key Support Question 7—What ACTIONS am I willing to take, to get the support I need?

If you want to be average, all you have to do is sit around, whine, and complain. Unsuccessful people complain that the world isn't supporting them enough. On the other hand, Three Percenters shut up, get to work, and show other people how they will benefit from supporting *them*.

What are you going to do differently to get the support you need? Do everything you can think of; the crazier the better. Hey, if what you've been doing up until now worked, you'd already be successful! By definition, therefore, what seems crazy to you might be the one action that makes all the difference.

INTERVIEW TIME

After you answer the seven Key Support Questions, it's time to do something with the information you learned. Earlier, I mentioned that you need to find Loving Mirrors for your life and Safe Havens for your business. Well, here's where we're going to do it.

Now, I could just tell you to walk up to your potential Loving Mirrors and talk to them. But, what would you say? You don't think I'd leave you hanging like that, do you? Instead, I'm handing you the script so you don't have to worry about what to say. You can be as transparent as this and say to your friend:

"You're a very important person to me. I'm making some big changes in my life, and I'd like you to be a part of it. I'm reading a book by this guy Noah St. John, and he told us to interview the most important people in our lives, because he said that the most successful people have other people who believe in them."

Your friend might say, "What are you talking about?" so just explain it simply and honestly. Tell them that these are the questions you are supposed to ask.

Let them know exactly what you're doing. Tell them, "I want to make some big changes, and you're an important part of that. I was wondering if I could ask you these questions. Is that okay with you?"

What are they going to say? "No, I don't want to talk to you because you just made me feel good!"?

Wouldn't *you* like it if somebody said something like this to you? "You mean you care about *me*? You *value* me?" By the way, I can pretty much guarantee that no one has ever said this to them.

Think about it: When was the last time someone said something like this to *you*?

You can do this on the phone or in person; you can go out for coffee, lunch, or just hang out. Many of my Students have done this via email, because naturally, you can have Loving Mirrors and Safe Havens on the other side of the world just as easily as in your hometown. That's fine, too.

So, here's your script. You don't have to reinvent the wheel. It's right here.

EXERCISE: INTERVIEW YOUR LOVING MIRRORS AND SAFE HAVENS

1. What do you get out of me being in your life?

2. What have you *gained* from our relationship? Please be specific.

3. What would be *missing* if I weren't in your life?

4. What do you see as my *strengths*?

5. What can I do *differently* to improve our relationship?

6. If there were one word or phrase you'd use to describe our relationship, what would it be?

7. On a scale of 1 to 10, how would you rate our relationship?

8. (If anything less than 10) What can I do to make it a 10?

These questions are very straightforward, but I do want to highlight questions 7 and 8. Jack Canfield taught me these, and they are two of the most brilliant questions I've ever seen in human relations.

Question 7: "On a scale of 1 to 10, how would you rate our relationship?" Ask, then listen. If their answer is anything less than a 10, then you need to ask Question 8: "What can I do to make it a 10?"

Jack often says that he and his wife ask each other these two questions every week, whether he's calling from Kuala Lumpur or at home with his family. They take the time to ask each other these questions—"On a scale of 1 to 10, how would you rate our relationship?" and "What can I do to make it a 10?"

Can you imagine how close, how loving their relationship is? They're both taking the time to ask, "What can I do to make this a better relationship?" Who does this? It's staggering.

If you're in business, I highly recommend that you ask your team, department, employees, and even your vendors these two questions. Go to every important person in your organization and say, "Let's do this. Let's get to a 10." You will have just earned their loyalty.

WHERE YOU COME FROM

I don't mean where you were born. I mean that, when you're doing this process, *where you come from is even more important than the questions you ask.* You must come from a place of authenticity, not need.

You can't defend. Why? Because when you defend, you lose. For example, let's say you ask someone, "On a scale of 1 to 10, where would you rate our relationship?" and she answers, "It's a four." You react defensively: "A four! What are you talking about? I'm always doing stuff for you, and I'm always nice to you . . ." If you do that, you've just lost.

Although you may not like to hear what she's saying, you've got to suck it up. Take a deep breath. Calmly say, "Wow, a four. That's not very good. So, what's going on that I don't know about?"

See what you did there? You gave the other person *permission to tell you the truth.* She might say, "Well, you never listen to me. You interrupt me all the time, and you didn't let me finish telling you that story . . ." This is your moment of truth. If you can let her tell *her* truth without defending yourself, then you've won.

The #1 thing human beings are silently aching for is simply to be heard—and not be made wrong.

Everyone is dying to tell their story. What if you became the one person who doesn't make them wrong for it?

You don't have to agree with everything that everyone says. But you don't have to make them wrong, either. All you are doing is listening. You can say something like, "Wow, I had no idea I was doing that. I'm sorry. I'll do better next time." (And it's even better if you mean it.)

THE END OF EXCUSES

You can have excuses or success—but not both. If you come in with your excuses, like, "I was sick that day, I wasn't feeling well, somebody did this to me when I was six years old," you've just diminished yourself in that person's eyes and you lost that opportunity to grow.

Everybody's got excuses. Unsuccessful people are whiners and victims. Don't be one of them! Say, "Wow, I didn't know I was doing so poorly. What can I do to make it better?"

On the other hand, you might be pleasantly surprised. Maybe the person you ask says that your relationship's a 9. Then, you can say, "Wow, a 9 is pretty good. What can I do to make it a 10?"

Give people permission to give you their honest answer. Then, you'll have that confidence to know, hey, I can do better next time. Give people permission to be truthful with you this time, and you'll find they're more likely to support you next time.

A FINAL WHY-TO

Finding your Loving Mirrors and Safe Havens comes with one additional Benefit: Every other success program implicitly tells you to go to yourself to find the strength to complete it. However, the very point is that most of us don't believe in ourselves enough to finish what we start!

When you gain unconditional support from others, this ensures that you no longer need to depend on your own willpower to get your foot off the brake. Therefore, if you find yourself getting stuck in your life or business at any time in the future, simply go back to this Step and do the exercises again. I have found, in working with thousands of Students, that as we let ourselves succeed at higher and higher levels, we consistently need to shore up the support that got us there. *The Secret Code of Success,* therefore, is the only personal improvement System with the failsafe Step built right into it.

When you do this Step, you won't have to depend on your own willpower or "psych yourself up" anymore. Because, as we've seen, those are very limited resources to begin with. Now, you can simply do what the Three Percenters have been unconsciously doing all along—letting other people believe in you, and allowing them to support you on your journey to a richer, happier life.

A QUICK RECAP

1. Just like you can't see your own eyes by looking from within yourself, you cannot determine, or even understand, your own value by looking to yourself. That's why you need the *unconditional support* of other people to become the person you were meant to be.

2. Loving Mirrors are people who give you unconditional support in your personal life, and **Safe Havens** support you in your professional life. The main difference is that a Safe Haven sees your personal potential while holding you accountable to the demands of business.

3. The **Loving Mirror Principle** flips traditional success literature on its head, because the traditional teachers have told you to "believe in yourself." The truth is, believing in yourself is the last thing that happens. Before you can ever believe in yourself, you must have someone else believe in you.

4. Do the exercises in this chapter to find your Loving Mirrors and Safe Havens. This will be a lifelong process. Most people (including the author) started this process with no Loving Mirrors or Safe Havens. However, keep focusing on what's right with the people in your life, and you will begin to attract the kind of people who can support you in your journey to Success.

Next Actions: List three things you can do from this chapter in the next seven days to gain and give a more fulfilling level of unconditional support for your life and business.

1._____

2._____

3._____

TOP 10 AFFORMATIONS FOR STEP 2:

1. Why do I have so many Loving Mirrors in my life?

2. Why do I have so many Safe Havens in my business?

3. Why am I a Loving Mirror and Safe Haven to the people in my life?

4. Why do I take responsibility for gaining the support I need to succeed?

5. Why do I have the courage to ask for the support I need?

6. Why am I always in the right place at the right time with the right people?

7. Why do I gain and give support in equal measure?

8. Why do so many great people support me?

9. Why do I attract so many leaders to my business?

10. Why do I have permission to be Who I Really Am?

CHAPTER 6

Step 3: Systems of Support

**"Put a good person in a bad System, and
the System will win every time."**

—W. EDWARDS DEMING

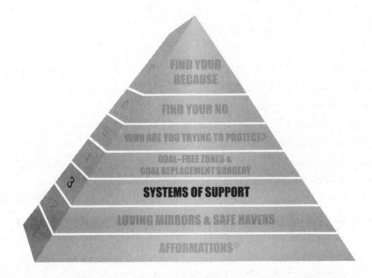

Think about your house. What *is* your house, really? At its core,
your house consists of two things—**Structure** and **Systems**. Your
house's Structure is its particular style—Cape, Ranch, Victorian,
etc.—and includes how its individual parts are arranged: number
of rooms, sizes of the rooms, where they're placed, and so on. Your
house's Structure is its parts.

Secondly, your house consists of Systems. Systems make your house's parts serve a function. Your house's Systems include: electric, heating, ventilation, plumbing, and so forth. These Systems give you a space in which you can live comfortably. That is the function of a house. If your house's Systems don't work properly, you've got a building sitting there that's not much fun to live in.

When is the only time you ever think about the Systems in your house? Exactly: when they break. You only think about a System in your house when it's not working. The only time you ever think about your plumbing is when your drain gets stopped up. You never think about electricity until you go to turn on a light and nothing happens.

Think about your body. Your body is like a house, because your body is also composed of Structure and Systems. The Structure is your basic makeup: male or female, tall or short, and your individual features and genetic characteristics.

Then, you have Systems. The function of your body's Systems is for you to remain alive. Your body contains dozens of interdependent Systems: circulatory, muscular, skeletal, nervous, respiratory, immune . . . plumbing! When do you ever think about these Systems? You got it: when they break. You never think about your respiratory system unless you suddenly can't breathe; or your digestive system until you're in the doctor's office saying, "Gee, maybe I shouldn't have eaten those 15 chocolate donuts . . ."

As you can see, if your house's or body's Systems aren't working at optimal levels, you have a bunch of parts that don't serve the function you want. Well, it's the same with your life and your business.

Your life and your business also consist of Structure and Systems. But here's where we run into . . .

THE TWO THINGS MISSING FROM MOST PEOPLE'S LIVES AND BUSINESSES

1. Most people have no idea what the Systems of their lives and businesses are; and

2. Almost no one knows how to fix these Systems when they're broken.

Most people are doing something like this: *"Oh my God! I'm so overwhelmed. I don't know what to do! I've got too much to do and too little time. I'm broke! I've got no money. I'm overweight. What am I gonna do?"*

What is the *function* of your *life*? Of your business? Most people have never asked these simple, but essential questions. In fact, they don't even know what the question is, let alone how to answer it.

After working with tens of thousands of grateful Students, I've come to realize something both profound and simple. I'm not trying to tell you the meaning of life, but it seems that the highest function of an individual's life is *to live in the manner in which you choose.* That means to be able to choose the life you really want.

And the function of a business? The essential function of a business is *to provide value to a set of human beings and realize a profit from that activity.*

As you can see from the two descriptions, many people are not living what could be called an optimal life, and most businesses are certainly not functioning at optimal levels. Most people have a vague sense of this, and are running around trying to "fix" the problem. But if you were having a plumbing problem in your house (or body!), and kept calling an electrician, how successful would that operation be?

Take a deep breath. You can stop running around now. That's because, after working with countless Students in my mentoring programs and studying the world's happy, successful people, I've identified the five essential Systems that you need to be operating properly, to have a life and a business that perform the functions you want.

THE FIVE ESSENTIAL SYSTEMS OF SUPPORT™

System 1 is your **People System.**

System 2 is your **Activities System.**

System 3 is your **Environment System.**

System 4 is your **Introspection System.**

System 5 is your **Simplify System.**

People, Activities, Environment, Introspection, and *Simplify.* Those are the five Systems of Support in your life and in your business or career. You'll notice, as we discuss each one, that the same Systems that need to be working properly in your life also need to be working properly in your business. This is handy, because it means we can study the exact same Systems for both.

I don't care what business you're in, or whether you're an entrepreneur or work for someone else. The Systems are the same. I have consulted for scores of different industries, worked with tens of thousands of people in my seminars, and studied firsthand countless mega-successful individuals. It simply doesn't matter who you are, what you do, or what business you're in; the Systems are the same.

That means, however, that if one of these five essential Systems is not working properly in your life or your business, not only will your income suffer, but your peace of mind, health, well-being and relationships will also suffer. You may notice this as a vague sense of "something's wrong," but you may have been unable to pinpoint exactly what it is. As we go through each System, you'll see not only what's wrong, but precisely how to fix it.

PRACTICE MAKES . . .

The pain and confusion of "something's wrong, but I don't know what it is" can be avoided when you know what the Systems are, and then take steps to make them work at higher and more effective levels. Remember, this is a course of ACTION, but it's also a *process*. Practice does not make perfect; *practice makes progress*. The word *progress* comes from the Latin *progredi*, which means "to step forward." Life is not about being perfect; it's about having the courage to move forward, one step at a time.

Before we start, I want you to do something for me right now. Take a deep breath. Now, one more deep breath. As you're reading these words, become aware of your heartbeat. Sit quietly for a moment. Can you feel your heartbeat?

Put your finger on your throat where you get a strong pulse, or just feel your heartbeat inside your body. Breathe. Now . . .

When was the last time you thought about your heart beating? Seriously. When was the last time you thought about that? I bet you've almost *never* thought about it, unless you'd had a heart attack or some kind of chest pain.

When was the last time you thought about the fact that you digest food? Have you *ever* thought about that? Every day, three times a day (or more), we put a bunch of stuff in our mouths; but what happens once it's in there?

We live, breathe, eat, walk around, work, play, jog, and do whatever we want . . . and we never think about these incredible Systems that are right here in our amazing body, this singular temple.

STOP DISSING YOUR SYSTEMS

Instead of cherishing this amazing gift of our body, most of us ignore it, abuse it, or beat ourselves up about it. *"I'm too fat. I can't lose twenty pounds. I wish I had more hair on my head and not everywhere else. I wish I looked ten years younger."*

We're constantly beating up this miraculous body temple we have. I want you to realize that there are so many Systems functioning in our bodies that we never even think about. In fact, we totally disrespect them.

Next time you eat, try to force yourself to digest your food. If you had to sit there and make your body digest food, you'd starve to death! Try to make your heart beat. You can't; it just happens.

These Systems are working on their own, whether or not you are aware of them. It's the same in our lives and businesses. The five essential Systems of Support operate whether we like it, whether we ignore them, or whether we abuse them. (Of course, it's the same with our lovely little planet. Only now are we beginning to realize how much damage we've inflicted to the precious, and surprisingly fragile, Systems of Earth. That's why we must act now if we want them to continue to function properly and support a life that's livable for all of us.)

The Three Percenters tend to have Systems that function beautifully in their lives and businesses. But here's the maddening thing: they usually don't know what they did! Nevertheless, their Systems are functioning at or near optimal levels. Once you learn what the Systems are and how to make them work properly, you can do what they do, too.

You may be thinking that nothing is working in your life right now. But as we go through the five essential Systems, you may be pleasantly surprised to see that more is going *right* in your life than is going *wrong*. Then, you can simply take the ACTIONS suggested here to fix what's wrong and strengthen what's right.

YOUR PEOPLE SYSTEM

We start with the **People System**. Why is the People System the most essential System of Support? Because if your People System is not operating properly, nothing else matters. You simply won't succeed to your full potential without installing your People System at its optimal level.

Why? Well, there are many reasons, but the bottom line is this: *because people have all the money.* If you're trying to form a career or build a business, and humans aren't buying your stuff, I'm not exactly sure how you're going to make money. As far as we know, dolphins, monkeys, and gorillas are not carrying credit cards. (And my name is Noah, so I should know these things.)

> **$20 bills tend to NOT walk down the street, knock on your door and say, "Hey, can I come in?" If they do where you live, I want to live where you live!**

On the planet Earth, money comes attached to these strange things called "human beings"—and we have to do that annoying thing called "work" to have money be transferred from their wallet to yours. Therefore, if you want to have more of the thing called money, you'd better install your People System.

THE FIVE A'S OF YOUR PEOPLE SYSTEM

There are five ACTIONS, that all happen to start with the letter A that you must master to properly install your People System. The five A's of your People System are:

1. Acknowledge

2. Ask

3. Accept

4. Accountability

5. Afform

People System First A = Acknowledge

The first A of your People System is **Acknowledge**. Why is that the first A of your People System? Because human beings (you know, those weird things with all the money?) are starving for attention, appreciation, recognition, and acknowledgement. Research has shown that people will do more for acknowledgement than for money. Who would you rather work for: someone who pays you a million dollars a year but demeans, embarrasses, and humiliates you; or someone who pays you a hundred thousand dollars a year but who praises, acknowledges, and appreciates you?

Sure, you might work for the first boss for a while; but you'd look at that paycheck every month and ask yourself, "Is this really worth it?" We humans are strange creatures. We think we want money (and we do); but many people are shackled by "the golden handcuffs" and "stuck" in high-paying, low-fulfilling jobs.

There are dozens of ways to Acknowledge the people in your life, at work, and at home. What it really comes down to, though, is your willingness to do so. That's because every one of us is wearing an invisible sign that says, "Please make me feel important." The problem is, you have that sign too! That's why everyone is waiting for *someone else* to make them feel important *first*, before they're willing to do it for others.

If you can be that one person in a million (and this number is pretty accurate) who Acknowledges other people first, you are on your way to optimally installing your People System.

People System Second A = Ask

Imagine that you and I are in a big room with hundreds of other *Secret Code of Success* Students, gathered together to study these principles. Of course, this is exactly what happens in our seminars, so it's not too difficult to imagine!

Would you find it difficult to ask the people in this room for support? Would you feel embarrassed, shy, or hesitant to ask people for the support you need?

When I ask my seminar audiences if they find it hard to ask for the support they need, *even from people that they know*, more than 70 percent say yes. Why are we so afraid to ask? It all comes down to . . .

A FOUR-LETTER WORD STARTING WITH F

That word is, of course, *fear*. (What word were YOU thinking about?)

What causes the fear of asking? It's really the *fear of rejection*. It's the fear that the other person might say no; the fear that someone might laugh at us or make fun of us. This fear may stem from when we were told, "Shut up, go away and don't bother me." Maybe not in so many words, but we got the point.

Many of us have that background where we were essentially told to go away. We took that with us as adults, and we continued to believe that's how life is. I invite you to notice that very successful people do not have a problem asking. You've heard that the best salespeople keep asking for the sale. Not that they are hounding people; they simply keep asking.

There's a huge difference between hounding and asking. You might say, "I don't want to be rude. I don't want to bother people." And you are right: you shouldn't be rude or bother people. But what if you're presenting an opportunity that would truly benefit that other person? If you're adding value to others, don't you owe it to them, and to yourself, to at least ask if they're interested?

A few years ago, a friend who'd taken my seminars told me that the company she worked for really needed my help. She gave me a person to call at the company's headquarters, the head of convention services. When I told this person what my friend had said, she replied, "No, thanks. We're all set." Click.

That was weird, I thought. Maybe I caught her on a bad day.

So I called back a month or two later just to check in. "No, thanks." Same response.

This actually happened a couple more times until I got a clue. I called my friend back and asked, "Are you sure I'm talking with the right person?" She gave me another name, this time a vice president who oversaw the company's regional conventions. I dialed, fully prepared to be shot down again. The VP asked me what I did. I said, I show people how to get rid of their head trash. She asked me how my System worked. I told her about the results people were getting in a matter of weeks, even days.

She said, "That sounds good. Let me have someone call you back." *Yeah, right,* I thought.

The next day, I got in to work and there was a message: "Noah, this is ____. I just spoke with our VP and we'd like you to speak on a cruise to Mexico for two thousand of our international salespeople. We'll fly you first class to Los Angeles and you'll have to speak for a couple of hours. You can relax for the rest of the four-day cruise. Oh, and we're putting you in one of the master cabins on the ship and will pay for everything."

All righty then.

My point: If I had stopped at the first "no," I wouldn't have flown first class and stayed in a master cabin on a cruise ship to Mexico, and get paid to do what I love. However, I didn't keep asking the wrong person when that wasn't getting the result I wanted.

Many teachers talk about how important it is to keep asking and be persistent. But the point they missed is that *persistence is a behavior*. As we learned in an earlier chapter, behavior cannot be created at the level of behavior. Therefore, to create *the behavior of persistence*, you must find your deeper Why-To. To gain the courage to Ask, you must understand the value you bring to others.

One reason our company has grown so quickly is because we're ridiculously clear about the value we bring to people. People who want that value come to us—and tell their friends to buy from us, too. Here's what we do at SuccessClinic.com:

> **"We teach people how to get their foot off the brake in their lives, careers and relationships— and show them the Steps to double their income in 90 days while working *less*."**

If you want that, come to us. If you don't want that, don't come to us.

Now, it's one thing to go around saying stuff like that, and quite another to prove it. We have unassailable proof that our System works. Not only do lots of famous people endorse our System, but regular people like you and me tell their personal stories of how they've doubled, tripled, even *quintupled* their incomes in less than 180 days because of what they learned from us.

You can do this, too. Present your value to others, Ask if they're interested, and if they say no . . . so what? You're no worse off than you were before you asked. You already didn't have the thing, right? So you haven't lost anything, have you?

And, who knows . . . keep presenting your value to others, and one day, the right person will say yes.

People System Third A = Accept

The third A in your People System is to **Accept**. This is a very subtle, but oh so powerful concept. When I first started teaching this System ten years ago, I was teaching people to Acknowledge and Ask, but I felt like something was missing because people kept getting stuck at this level. Finally, I realized what was wrong.

I saw that people were missing this powerful but subtle concept, which is to *accept support from other people*. It sounds bizarre, but many people can't Accept the support that's right in front of their faces. Ironically, to Accept support is actually a higher level than to Ask for support—and I'll prove it to you.

Think about a time when you had a birthday, anniversary, or holiday where you received gifts. Have you ever received a gift that was better than anything you asked for? Something better than anything you dared to ask for? When I ask this question in my seminars, nearly every hand goes up, because this has happened to nearly everyone at least once.

That's why to Accept support really is a higher level than to Ask for it. You can ask for something, and still not let yourself receive it. Conversely, you may not ask for something and get it anyway! However, many people have a hard time accepting support, love, and encouragement from others.

You may be unwittingly pushing support away. Of course you don't mean to do this; but this is one of the jobs of your Negative Reflection, which tells you that you don't deserve to be supported anyway, so why bother?

Sometimes, you simply have to breathe to let others support you. There's no big secret to Accepting support, but realize that this might be a big hidden block for you. Write in your *Secret Code of Success Journal* about this, and stop pushing people's support away.

People System Fourth A = Accountability

Have you ever noticed that we'll do more for other people than we will for ourselves?

Go to **www.SecretCodeBook.com** and watch the "Death Crawl" clip from *Facing the Giants*. What's so powerful about this clip is that Brock wouldn't have made the crawl on his own. He didn't want to let his coach or the other players down, and so he made it all the way across the field with a man on his back. Left to his own devices, do you really think Brock would have pushed himself that far?

That's why, when you are **Accountable** to someone else, you will soon be pleasantly surprised to see that you can do far more than you knew you could.

In traditional success programs, they told us, *"Think about all the money you're going to make! Think about the new car! Think about how rich you'll be!"* and so on.

They told us to visualize the things we'll have when we're successful, and told us that would motivate us to take action. So, why that didn't work for most of us?

We think we want things. But really, it's EXPERIENCES we want.

It's not the Ferrari we want; we want the *feeling of specialness and importance* we think the Ferrari will give us. It's not the mansion or yacht; it's the *feeling of being rich.*

Sure, we all want nicer things like cars, houses, and our own island in the Caribbean. But after working with tens of thousands of people in my seminars and interviewing scores of multi-millionaire mega-successes, I have found, ironically, that the two essential experiences we human beings want are *significance* and *contribution.*

We want to *feel significant* to other people, and we want *the feeling that we made a difference.* Sure, we want a billion dollars, and there's nothing wrong with having lots of money. But each of my multi-millionaire friends has told me, without fail, that after the cars, the vacations, and private jets, they kept asking themselves: *"Is this all there is? What significance do I have? Have I really made a difference on this Earth?"*

Therefore, rather than waiting until you're "successful," start asking those questions now—when the money starts pouring in, you'll already have arrived.

People System Fifth A = Afform

Remember how I taught you about Afformations—the empowering questions that change your life? Well, here's where you can start to use them to create the life you really want.

We've been taught to affirm what we want by saying affirmations; but as I showed you in Step 1, most of us don't believe these positive things we say. With Afformations, rather than bang your head against your own brain, you can simply use your mind to manifest the things you want twice as fast with half the effort.

One of my Students had spent a lot of time, money, and energy on every weight-loss program out there, but she still couldn't lose the weight she wanted. After she heard me teach about Afformations, she realized that she was unconsciously asking herself disempowering questions like, *"Why can't I lose weight? Why am I so fat? Why don't these work for me?"* Can you guess why she wasn't succeeding at what she wanted?

After learning how to create empowering Afformations, she started asking: *"Why do I lose weight so easily?"* She began using the four Steps of The Afformations Method I showed you in Step 1. She didn't just ask the question; she gave herself to the question, and took action.

After about sixty days, she realized that she not only felt better, but her clothes fit better. She got on a scale and it showed that she had lost twenty pounds! But here's the amazing thing: *She didn't believe it.*

Because she really hadn't worked hard, or dieted, or stressed about it, she couldn't see how she'd lost all that weight almost without effort. So she went to her mom's house and checked the scale there. It showed the same thing: she'd lost twenty pounds. *Well,* she thought, *that scale must be broken, too.*

Finally, she went to her doctor and got on the scale at the doctor's office, because that scale had to be working. The scale at the doctor's confirmed what she herself didn't even believe: She had lost twenty pounds in sixty days without stress or dieting.

What I think is so amazing about this story isn't even that she lost all that weight. The amazing part is she didn't believe her own results, because they had come "too easily." How's that for manifesting?

The moral of the story? Don't affirm—Afform for the life you really want—and then let yourself enjoy it!

EXERCISE: INSTALLING THE FIVE A'S OF YOUR PEOPLE SYSTEM

1. Who do I need to **Acknowledge** for their contribution to my life?

2. What ACTIONS can I take to Acknowledge them today?

3. What ACTIONS can I take to Acknowledge them consistently?

4. Assuming I'm not afraid of the answer, who would I **Ask** for their support?

5. What can I do to **Accept** the support of people who want me to succeed?

6. Who can I be **Accountable** to, for my Success?

7. What will happen if I don't feel Accountable to someone for my Success?

8. What are my top 10 **Afformations** I can use to install my People System?

YOUR ACTIVITIES SYSTEM

The next System of Support is your **Activities System**. This is how you spend the hours and days of your life. I know it sounds simple, but we live our lives in days. Not weeks, not months, not years; but days. If you feel out of control, if you have "too much to do and too little time," there are two simple questions that can transform the days of your life and explode your personal productivity.

EXERCISE: THE TWO QUESTIONS THAT CAN EXPLODE YOUR PRODUCTIVITY

Column A	Column B
What would I love to do *more* of?	What would I love to do *less* of?
(Activities that *Fill My Tank*)	(Activities that *Empty My Tank*)

In Column A, list your answers to: "What would I love to do *more* of?" This is a list of activities that **Fill Your Tank.** In Column B, answer, "What would I love to do *less* of?" These are the activities that **Empty Your Tank.**

By the way, did you notice that to *fill your tank* and *empty your tank* are success clichés? You didn't think I was going to let myself get away with that, did you? By now, you should know that I'm here to bust traditional success clichés. We've heard these phrases a million times; but what does it really mean to *fill your tank* and *empty your tank?*

YOUR THREE HUMAN RESOURCES

There are three resources or commodities that we can use as human beings. They are: time, energy, and money. That's all we have on the Earth. Of our three human resources, which do you think is the most valuable?

Some people say energy is the most valuable, because all things are energy. Your body, your computer, your coffee mug; anything you and I can touch in the universe is energy. All things are made of molecules, molecules are made of atoms, and atoms are energy. We learned in high school that energy is infinite. Energy can be neither created nor destroyed; it just *is*. Since energy is infinite, it can't be the most valuable commodity.

What about money? Money is just a form of energy. The way money works is, you have some and everyone else has all the rest! Since money is just a form of energy, money is also, for all intents and purposes, infinite. Therefore, money can't be the most valuable commodity either.

The reason time is the most valuable human commodity is because *it is the only resource that can never be replaced.*

**All of Bill Gates' billions can't buy
one minute of yesterday.**

Therefore, when we talk about how to *fill your tank*, we're talking about activities that give you more of your human resources of time, energy, and money. And when you *empty your tank*, it means activities that *take away* one or more of your three human resources.

You may be thinking, "But Noah, you just said that I can't get more time. So, how can filling my tank mean I get more time?" Good catch. The fact is, you can't get more time; but you can create either more *productive time* or more *unproductive time*. *Productive time* means doing activities that move you toward what you want. *Unproductive time* means you are either doing activities that do not move toward what you want, or actually move you away from what you want.

For example, you might say you want to lose weight, but you spend all of your time sitting on the couch eating potato chips and watching TV. You're not using your resources very productively, now are you? You can't stay the same because all things deteriorate here on Earth; all things break down due to the physical law known as *entropy*.

That's why you're either moving toward something you want or you're not—that's productive or unproductive. That does NOT mean you should be working all the time. Productive time also includes taking *Goal-Free Zones*, which we'll talk about in Step 4.

For now, I'd like you to fill out those two columns above. Many times in my seminars when people do this Step, they're blown away by how much time they're spending on activities that empty their tank. Gee, I wonder why they feel like a failure?

Once you've filled out those columns, answer these questions:

EXERCISE: INSTALLING YOUR ACTIVITIES SYSTEM

1. What reasons (excuses) have I been giving for not doing the Activities in Column A?

2. When are those reasons (excuses) not valid?

3. What Activities can I DO from Column B (just get them over with)?

4. What Activities can I DELETE from Column B (just eliminate them)?

5. What Activities can I DELEGATE from Column B (let somebody else do them) and to whom?

6. What ACTIONS will I take to more productively use my time, energy and money—so I can do *more* of what fills my tank and *less* of what empties it?
   Daily Actions:

   Weekly Actions:

7. Who will I be Accountable to for reporting those Activities?

Column A includes activities that you'd love to do more of, activities that fill your tank. Most of us are saying, "I can't, I can't." So tell me: Why can't you? The reasons always boil down to, "I don't have the time, the money, or the energy." Hmm, interesting that it always comes down to our use of our three human commodities . . .

Look at the second question—When are those reasons (excuses) not valid? Notice that I keep using the word *excuses*. When are those reasons or excuses not valid? "I don't have the time." You do have the time. Think about it. Nobody has more time or less time than you do. Everyone has the same twenty-four hours in a day, and even Bill Gates hasn't figured out how to slow down the Earth's rotation (but I hear he's working on that).

Next time you hear yourself saying, "I don't have the time," I want you to realize that you just told a lie. It is a lie to say you don't have the time. If you say, "I'm choosing not to do that," or "That's not a priority for me right now"—now, you're telling the truth.

Whether or not you choose consciously, you're making a choice. Your choice may be valid, or your Negative Reflection may cause it. You need to figure out which is true.

For example, let's look at the excuse: "I don't have the money." Actually, the truth is you do have the money, but you're *choosing to allocate it for different things right now.* For example, did you know that you could own a Rolls Royce right now? Let me show you.

HOW TO OWN A ROLLS ROYCE RIGHT NOW

Let's say you own your home and have a monthly mortgage payment. A monthly car payment for a Rolls Royce might be about the same amount as your monthly mortgage payment. That means you actually do have the money for a Rolls Royce right now. The problem is, of course, that if you chose the Rolls, you might not be able to pay your house payment, too. So you'd have to live in your Rolls Royce. Probably not the best choice!

The point is, you are allocating money right now for the things that you have determined are a priority: say, food, clothing, and shelter. So, even though many people don't believe me when I say this, you do have the money for most of the things on your list.

THE 3-D WAY TO INCREASE PRODUCTIVITY

In questions 3, 4, and 5, we see that there are three things you can do with the Activities in Column B: you can *Do* them, *Delete* them, or *Delegate* them. *What can I do? What I can delete? And what can I delegate?*

Those are the three D's—**Do, Delete,** or **Delegate**—that we can do with anything that comes into our lives. In question 3, What Activities can I *Do* from Column B (just get them over with)? these are what you want to do less of and just get rid of. *"I'm sick of thinking about it. I don't want to do it, but I am going to just get it over with."* This might be bookkeeping, accounting, your newsletter or any number of other tedious-to-you Activities. Like swallowing your medicine or going to the dentist, sometimes it's best just to get them over with.

Question 4 is, What Activities can I *Delete* from Column B (just get rid of them)?" *"I'm not even going to do it. It's just not going to happen. Forget it; I want to take it off my plate."* These are the things you want to Delete.

Now, look at question 5: "What Activities can I *Delegate* from Column B and to whom?" *This is the key to maximum success with minimum effort.* The Three Percenters have mastered the vital skill of delegation.

If you want to truly increase your productivity, the most important D is to Delegate. Why? Because that's where you start to multiply your effectiveness and gain leverage in your life. This is what happy, rich people do. Happy, rich people gain great leverage by delegating.

Do you think Donald Trump goes around building all those big buildings? Uh, no. He goes around telling people, "Do this, this, and this," in his weird New York accent. He's a master delegator. Now, I'm not saying we have to be like Donald Trump; maybe for you, you need to delegate the laundry.

I have found delegating to be the hardest step for most entrepreneurs, because they either say, "I don't have anyone to delegate to," or because they don't trust anyone to do things "as well as they do." If that's your belief, you've just signed up for the Struggle Express.

In question 6, list what ACTIONS you can do to more productively use your three human resources. List the daily and weekly actions you can take to make better uses of your time, money, and energy. Why should you make this list? So you can do more of what you want to do and less of what you don't want to do!

The final question to install your Activities System is: *"Who will I be Accountable to for reporting these Activities?"* You may be accountable to your whole group, or just to one other person. You might say, "This is what I'm going to do. I'm going to Do, Delete, and Delegate at higher levels. If you catch me not doing this, I want you to call me on it." Give your people permission to catch you not doing this.

This is called *positive peer pressure*; telling everybody that you're going to do something positive. If you fall short, everyone will see that, and you'll be embarrassed. Since no one wants to be embarrassed (that's a big Why-Not-To), you will take action.

Ironically, with higher levels of Accountability, you are actually doing less and having more. Remember, the goal is maximum wealth with minimum effort. I don't know about you, but that sounds pretty good to me.

FINALLY, THE RIGHT TOOL

Over the last forty years, we've been inundated with time management tools of every kind. From Post-Its to planners to Palm Pilots, the market is flooded with tools and gizmos that have tried to help us become more productive.

The problem with traditional time-management tools, however, is this: they haven't made us much more productive, and they certainly haven't made our lives any easier. Think about it: are you working LESS than you were five years ago, or more? Are you spending LESS time doing email, answering messages, and trying to find information, or more? Are you finding it EASIER to manage all the information coming at you, or are you working harder than ever just to keep up?

The answer, for most of us, is: *Are you kidding?*

That's why we invented the **Freedom Power Pack**: a breakthrough in time management and productivity, because it not only looks at your life through the five essential Systems of Support, it also puts them in context within the 4R's of your life:

1. The ROLE in which you're working.

2. The RESULT you want to achieve.

3. The RESOURCES you'll need to do them.

4. The RELATIONSHIPS needed to provide any resources you don't have.

It also includes WHAT we need to do, WHY we need to do it, and HOW we'll pull it off. The Freedom Power Pack tracks all factors involved and helps to tell when we're on course and off course, and why and how to get back on track. You can learn how to get your own Freedom Power Pack in the Additional Resources section at the back of this book.

YOUR ENVIRONMENT SYSTEM

Your third System of Support is your **Environment System**. You live in two environments—your **Outer Environment** and your **Inner Environment**. Your *Outer Environment* consists of your *Home Environment* and *Work Environment;* while your *Inner Environment* consists of your *Emotional Environment* and *Spiritual Environment*.

YOUR QUALITY OF LIFE

Your Outer Environment is the physical environment you can see and touch. You can't see your Inner Environment directly; you can only see the effects of it. Remember, the only two things that determine your quality of life are the quality of your communication with the world *outside of you,* and the quality of your communication with the world *inside of you.*

We live in two worlds. We experience our Outer Environment, but who's the experiencer? You. You experience the Outer Environment through the Inner Environment with your emotions, spirit, soul, and mind.

GET OUT OF YOUR FAMILIAR ZONE

During my live seminars, I ask people, "How many people feel that clutter is a problem in your life?" About 75 percent of the hands go up. Why do we have such a problem with clutter? While I could give you a lot of surface answers, it always comes down to *fear.* Fear keeps us in our **Familiar Zone**. You've heard a million times that you need to "get out of your comfort zone." But consider this:

Let's say you're driving down the road of life with one foot on the brake. You're aware that you're holding yourself back, and you don't like it. You wouldn't be reading this book if that weren't true.

Now, here's my question to you: Is that feeling *comfortable*? Is the feeling of going down the road of life with your foot on the brake comfortable?

You and I both know that it isn't comfortable at all. In fact, it's decidedly UNcomfortable. It is, however, familiar. When you look at that word *familiar,* what does that word look like to you?

Right—*family. Family* is the root of the word *familiar.* Some people in my seminars say "family-liar!" The point is:

You don't need to break out of your comfort zone—because your "comfort zone" doesn't exist. You need to break out of your Familiar Zone.

You may be *familiar* with clutter. You may be *familiar* with holding yourself back. You may be *familiar* with stopping yourself from success. In fact, it's certain that you are. But you're probably not very comfortable.

The purpose of this book and my teaching is to get you out of your Familiar Zone of pushing success away, and get you familiar—and finally, comfortable—with allowing yourself to succeed to your full potential.

CLEARING THE CLUTTER

I've always said that if I ever got into another business, it would be the self-storage business. Why? Because people are obsessed with buying stuff! And when there's too much stuff in the house, do they get rid of it? No, they get another storage unit. You can't even get the car in the garage—your poor car has to sit outside because you've got so much stuff in the garage. If this sounds familiar to you, you're not only in good company, you're in the vast majority.

Why do we need to get rid of clutter? The essential reason is that if you have physical or emotional clutter—meaning inner or outer clutter—it is very difficult for something better to come in. That is just another one of those laws of the universe. I didn't make this up; I just report the facts.

Have you ever noticed that when you clear stuff out, you feel better? I know you've noticed this. After one of my Students cleared the clutter from her Outer Environment and Inner Environment, she told me that her business doubled in just three weeks!

Another one of my clients couldn't see the rug in her office because she had so much clutter. When she cleaned out the clutter, she told me she took out *seventeen garbage bags* of clutter from her little office. Guess what? In thirty days, she made enough extra money in her business to replace the carpet that she couldn't see before.

Clearing the clutter works. Just accept it—and use it for your ultimate Benefit.

EXERCISE: INSTALLING YOUR ENVIRONMENT SYSTEM

1. What are the biggest blocks in my Home Environment?

2. What are the biggest blocks in my Work Environment?

3. What are the biggest blocks in my Emotional Environment?

4. What are the biggest blocks in my Spiritual Environment?

5. What ACTIONS can I take this week to clear the clutter from my Outer Environment?

6. What ACTIONS can I take this week to clear the clutter from my Inner Environment?

Environment System Questions 1 & 2—What are the biggest blocks in my Home and Work Environments?

You can write down ten, twenty, or more blocks. Be honest about what your biggest blocks are in your Outer Environment. In your Home Environment, it may be the squeaky door, the window that has to be replaced. *"The stairs are a problem. I can't get into my garage."* Whatever your blocks are—and you know what they are—write them down.

What about your Work Environment? *"I can't find my papers. I don't have the right software. I don't know where my computer is. I have an old computer that doesn't work properly."*

And clutter doesn't just mean a bunch of junk. It might mean that you need tools you don't currently have. Would you expect to build a nice house with just a hammer, a screwdriver, and two nails? You need all the correct tools and materials to do the job.

If you need a laptop, software, an assistant, a new phone, or any other tools, those could be some of your biggest roadblocks. Write what's missing that you know you need.

Your head trash is going to say, "I don't have the money!" What else is new? Just write it down anyway.

Environment System Questions 3 & 4—What are the biggest blocks in my Emotional and Spiritual Environments?

The two biggest pieces of emotional clutter are **fear** and **resentment**. *Fear* is about the future; *resentment* is about the past.

A lot of people say we have one foot in the past and one foot in the future, and you know what we're doing on our present. What are your biggest blocks in your Emotional Environment?

Then, what are the biggest blocks in your Spiritual Environment? For most people, their biggest spiritual block is: *They don't believe that miracles can happen for them.* They have lost their connection to God or something greater than themselves. They believe, "God has forsaken me because I've lost so much. I've done so many dumb things. God has forgotten about me."

Just because you've lost something—and you may have lost something or someone who was very, very special to you—that does not mean that God doesn't love you. We humans experience gain and loss; but to God, it's just What Is. God can't lose anything, and God can't gain anything. How could the Creator of this universe gain or lose anything?

We humans experience gain and loss, and we just happen to like gain better. When things are good, we say, "Thank you, God!" When we lose things, we say, "God, why did you do that to me?"

God is complete and perfect Unconditional Love, no matter what we humans experience. We think our experiences determine God's Love, but that's not how God looks at it. It's very difficult for us as human beings to understand how God Loves, because God is perfect Unconditional Love—with a capital L. We humans can only love with conditional love—the lowercase l.

I don't care how nice, sweet, and wonderful you are; you love conditionally. Every one of us has conditions on our love, but God doesn't. Can you see how this can be a huge block in your Spiritual Environment?

That's why I want you to begin to believe that miracles can happen for you, too—not just for other people. I want you to realize that, not only can miracles occur for you, the fact is: *you are a miracle.*

Look around the universe. Look at the other planets, the solar system. Where else do you see life, let alone human life?

This planet has it all. That's why we have to work very hard right now to protect it. Do you know what a miracle it is that life exists? If we could only carry that sense of awe with us all the time, you would experience and remember the miracle that life is.

Okay, you've identified the blocks in your Inner Environment and Outer Environment. Now, let's talk about the appropriate actions to clear the clutter.

Environment System Questions 5 & 6—What ACTIONS can I take to clear the clutter from my Inner and Outer Environments this week?

Many people ask me, "Noah, which should I start with—the Inner or the Outer?" I always tell them: "Start with the Outer." I know that sounds counterintuitive, because you say, "But I want to feel better on the inside!" Don't worry, you will.

Your Outer Environment includes the things you can see and touch. In case you haven't noticed, your Outer Environment greatly affects your emotional and spiritual well-being.

You can't find your papers. You're tripping over stuff. It's a mess. You have clutter. Isn't that frustrating? Darn right. Well, to be frustrated is a *feeling,* and feelings are caused by something. Therefore, when you remove the outer *cause* of the feeling, you will *feel better.*

So go through that closet, go through your files, clear off your desk and unload your inbox. Throw stuff away. You really don't need those bank records from twenty years ago.

My father is like this. He's a huge pack rat. I've told him over and over, "Dad, you really don't need those files from 1972." He doesn't want to let go, but I make, er, encourage him to toss them. And you know what? He always feels better afterward. (Why he doesn't remember that, remains a mystery.)

By the way, it's great to ask a friend to help you clear the clutter. Remember your People System? If you feel that you can't do it alone, ask a friend. Maybe it's one of your older kids, who's been saying, "Mom, Dad, when are you going to get rid of that junk?" Or, maybe your kid's house is neat because all of their junk is at your house! Call them and say, "Honey, I'm getting rid of your stuff on Sunday. Want to come over Saturday so you can take anything you still want?"

Don't feel that you have to do this alone. In fact, I highly suggest that you don't do it alone. Ask your Loving Mirrors at home and your Safe Havens at work for the support you need to succeed. Are you starting to get the order of this powerful System?

One final thought: Your Inner Environment and Outer Environment are not static and unchanging, but are vibrant and dynamic. Just because you cleared the clutter this week doesn't mean you won't have to do it again next week. One of my college professors was a Buddhist monk who said: "Half of life is cleaning." You eat dinner, you get dirty dishes. You clean them. You do it again tomorrow. That is called life.

YOUR INTROSPECTION SYSTEM

To *introspect* means "to look within." Why is that important? Simple: You need to determine whether your ladder of success is leaning against the wrong wall. You may be going after something you don't really want any more, or you may be going in a direction that is counter to the place you want to end up.

The world is a noisy place, and it's only getting noisier. When you walk in nature or go to the beach and you quietly look at the clouds, sand, trees, mountains, or water, have you ever noticed that you feel better?

I'm not saying you have to go to the mountains or the beach every day. I'm saying that you need to install your **Introspection System** in your life, to allow you to check your internal and external progress daily.

EXERCISE: INSTALLING YOUR INTROSPECTION SYSTEM

1. What ACTIONS can I do today that allow me to Introspect?

2. When is it easiest for me to do them?

3. What Successes did I have today?

4. What did I accomplish today that I'm proud of?

5. Am I going in the right direction? Is my company/team/career going in a direction I really want?

6. What ACTIONS can I do to get and keep us on track?

Yes, I know you're busy. Yes, I know you've got a million things to do today. So what makes you think that NOT introspecting will make your day and your life any easier?

Whether or not you like it, the Three Percenters find the time to Introspect daily, and they're just as busy as you are. They may not sit there and meditate (although many of them do), but they certainly have a System in place to ensure that they are going in the right direction.

WHAT NEEDS TO GET DONE, GETS DONE

Have you ever noticed that what needs to get done every day, gets done? Let's say you're going through your day as usual, when suddenly the phone rings. Someone says that your best friend is in the emergency room and you'd better get over there right now. Do you say, "Sorry, I'm too busy"? Or do you drop everything and rush to the ER?

Now, was "go to hospital" on your to-do list today? Of course not! But your Why-To's of being with your best friend outweighed your Why-Not-To's, and you acted on your true priorities.

You do not need or want to have an emergency to take care of something as important as yourself and your peace of mind. Most people are waiting for their lives to happen, then wondering why they're not happy or rich. If you don't install your Introspection System, the crush of information and to-do's can overwhelm even the most peaceful of us.

Daily Introspective exercises can include:

- ✔ Journaling
- ✔ Meditating
- ✔ Prayer
- ✔ Reading sacred literature
- ✔ Walking in nature
- ✔ Gardening

These are all ACTIONS that are Introspective because they allow you to look within and reconnect with your Authentic Self.

What can you do that allows you to get back in touch with

that still, small voice? That's your Authentic Self. Your Introspection System will allow you to get back in touch with your intuition, higher self, or whatever you wish to call it. This is part of all of us.

We've all had a hunch that turned out to be right. But how many times has the reverse happened? You do something, look back after the fact and say, "I *knew* I shouldn't have done that!" We've all done this. That's why we need to strengthen our connection to our Authentic Self—so we can make better choices in the moment of decision.

ACKNOWLEDGE YOUR SUCCESSES

Just as you're going to start Acknowledging others (your People System), guess what? You also need to Acknowledge *your own* successes. Most of us do the exact opposite and beat ourselves up for what we *didn't* do. We look at our to-do list and say, "Oh, I didn't do that and I didn't do that." Instead, Acknowledge the things you did.

Humans are motivated by success, not failure.

If you truly want to motivate yourself by what works, before you go to bed each night, Acknowledge the things you did right that day. Yes, you did a lot of things right today! Write them down, think about them, and focus on them.

What you focus on, grows. Most of us beat ourselves up for what we did "wrong." But if all you focus on is what you *don't* have, *haven't* done, and did "wrong," guess what you'll get more of? Why not do what you're already doing, but use it for your own benefit instead of beating yourself up more?

It's the little accomplishments that make a big difference. Acknowledge things you did, like, *"I made that tough phone call. I finished my newsletter. I followed up with that prospect. I organized that meeting."*

You can't control outcomes, but you can control your ACTIONS.

You can't control whether somebody buys your stuff or whether you get the promotion or a million other things. But, you can control what you do to influence those things, and your response to what happens.

And even if people say no, you can keep going—because that's what successful people do.

YOUR SIMPLIFY SYSTEM

When we look at the four preceding Systems—People, Activities, Environment, and Introspection—they lead to one natural, logical conclusion: the need to Simplify.

As I said before, the world is a noisy place and getting noisier. We don't live in the Information Age; we live in the Information Overload Age. There is simply too much information: too many interruptions, too many channels, too many emails. Ironically, when we have too many choices in life, our stress level goes up, because now we have the added stress of having to make the "right" choice!

I want you to write the following sentence in big letters, and put it by your desk where you'll see it every day:

SIMPLIFY YOUR LIFE, STREAMLINE YOUR BUSINESS

Let's say you're driving down the highway and decide you want something to eat. You see the golden arches and pull into a Mc-Donald's. You walk in and say you want a Big Mac. Does the 15-year-old behind the counter say, "Ooh, hold on a sec. How do we make a Big Mac again?"

Sure, people at fast food chains mess up, but there is a system that is both *streamlined* and *simple*. How do we know it's simple and streamlined? Because the result is the same no matter where in the world you go—and because it's often the first job the people who work there have ever held. While you can argue the quality of food, it's hard to argue with the success of such a streamlined operation.

Every successful company and organization has streamlined their Systems. Conversely, the individuals, teams, departments, companies, and organizations who haven't streamlined their Systems are not operating anywhere near full capacity or potential.

You can do this for your life and you can certainly do this in your business. And the place to start Simplifying is the process of delegating.

EXERCISE: INSTALLING YOUR SIMPLIFY SYSTEM

1. What tasks am I doing now that would I like to Delegate to someone else?

2. To whom would I like to Delegate those tasks?

3. What is My Win in the Delegation?

4. What is Their Win?

5. What is the Larger Win?

6. What ACTIONS can I do to Delegate today more than I did yesterday?

You might say, "But Noah, I don't have anyone to delegate to!" Yes, I've only heard that one a billion times, too. Well, for a long time, I didn't have anyone to delegate to, either. For me, just getting through the 2,517 emails I get per day was a huge time-sucking activity, and it was *emptying my tank*. Once I identified **My Win, Their Win,** and the **Larger Win,** I was finally able to Delegate that task—and my productivity went through the roof.

WIN X WIN X WIN = WIN³

You've heard of the concept of Win-Win, which means I Win and You Win, or mutual benefit. But there's another, higher level of negotiation, which I call **Win Cubed**—Win to the third power, Win^3. Win Cubed equals *Win times Win times Win*. It means I Win, You Win, and the World Wins. True leaders don't just focus on their Win and the other person's Win, but also the Win for the world.

Have you ever noticed that people will do more, and more willingly, when they believe they're contributing to a larger cause, a greater good or something bigger then themselves?

You've seen this in your own life and in the lives of the people around you. Why do you volunteer for things? Why do you donate to important causes? It's because you want to feel that you're contributing to something larger (remember that feeling of *contribution* and *significance* I talked about?). While you might not believe it, you can do this in your own business and your own life.

The people who I work with at The Success Clinic know that we are involved in something that's much bigger than any one of us, because our work allows us to contribute to the lives of countless numbers of people around the world. My job, as founder of the company, is to communicate that vision to the people who work with me, because they won't get that by osmosis or mind reading.

You, as the leader of your team, department, or organization, can do the same thing. You can communicate the larger Win to the people you work with and to whom you delegate, because the more everyone understands the bigger Win, the more energy they will give to everything they do.

For example, the mission of The Success Clinic is one sentence long. It reads:

We're creating a nation and a world of Loving Mirrors.

If you're excited about that, we want you on board. If not, then you're not the right person for our team.

If you're saying, "Well, I just want a paycheck," then frankly you won't be happy on our team. There's nothing wrong with wanting to collect a paycheck and go home. It's just that our team is comprised of people who are psyched about touching millions of lives and raising the consciousness of the Earth. If you want to be more successful, you need to communicate your vision with similar clarity.

I WIN, YOU WIN, THE WORLD WINS

Using my example of something as simple as email, I knew what task I wanted to delegate (**Simplify Question 1**). The problem was, I didn't have anyone to delegate that task to (**Simplify Question 2**).

I knew My Win would be that I'd get back many hours of my day I'd been spending on useless emails (**Simplify Question 3**). It felt like hours of my day were being taken from me. In addition, I felt exhausted and angry after trying to get through all those emails. I know you understand this! We're all faced with tasks that drain our time and energy.

So My Win was obvious and clear. Then, I determined Their Win (**Simplify Question 4**), even though I didn't have anyone at the time. I simply realized that, with the task of email, my new assistant's Win (whoever she was) would be: she'd get paid. Even before I found her, I determined that in receiving a good salary, she'd win.

Second, since I wouldn't have to read all that junk email, I would genuinely appreciate her. I remembered that most people will do more for appreciation than for money—although in this case, she'd get both.

Finally, I identified the Larger Win (**Simplify Question 5**). Because my new assistant would be contributing to helping me be more productive and happier, she would also know that we're now able to help more people and make a larger difference in the world. Therefore, when I delegate a task as seemingly innocuous as email, my time is freed, she gets the feeling of *significance* and *contribution*, and the world as a whole wins.

While you may think all this sounds rather grandiose, it works nonetheless. As a leader, you must communicate all three Wins to yourself and to your team. It's not other people's responsibility to determine Their Win or the Larger Win. Rich, happy people communicate all three Wins, whether or not they realize it. That's why they have so much of what the rest of the world wants.

You don't have to be a great public speaker or orator; but if you want to enjoy maximum wealth for minimum effort, you must understand and effectively communicate the three Wins not just to others, but also to yourself.

True wealth is much more than getting a bigger paycheck. While it's fine to want and get more money, true wealth means helping more people, touching more lives, and improving the world. That's why Simplifying Your Life and Streamlining Your Business—and installing all five essential Systems of Support—will enable you to enjoy more wealth and happiness with far less effort.

A QUICK RECAP

1. There are five essential **Systems of Support** that must operate properly for you to enjoy more wealth and happiness. Just like your house and your body, if these Systems aren't functioning optimally, you won't be very happy with the results.

2. The five Systems of Support are: **People, Activities, Environment, Introspection,** and **Simplify.** If one or more of these Systems is not operating optimally, your success and peace of mind will be quite limited.

3. Your **People System** consists of your ability to *Acknowledge, Ask, Accept, (have) Accountability,* and *Afform.*

4. Your **Activities System** means doing more of what fills your tank and less of what empties it.

5. Your **Environment System** means clearing the clutter from your Inner and Outer Environment.

6. Your **Introspection System** means doing daily exercises, such as meditation, prayer, or journaling that keep you on track toward what you really want.

7. Your **Simplify System** means to Simplify Your Life and Streamline Your Business. Simplifying and Streamlining are the hallmarks of a truly wealthy person and highly successful business. When you install the five essential Systems of Support at optimal levels in your life and your business, you'll enjoy more wealth and happiness using less time, money and effort than ever before.

Next Actions: List three things you can do from this chapter in the next seven days to install the five Systems of Support in your life and business.

1. _____

2. _____

3. _____

TOP 10 AFFORMATIONS FOR STEP 3:

1. Why do I have so much support in my life?

2. Why are leaders so magnetized to me?

3. Why do I take responsibility for doing things that fill my tank?

4. Why do I use my energy so effectively?

5. Why do I love throwing things away that no longer fit Who I Really Am?

6. Why do I enjoy keeping my Outer Environment clean?

7. Why do I love keeping my Inner Environment clear?

8. Why do I listen to my intuition when making big decisions?

9. Why do I take responsibility for simplifying my life?

10. Why do I enjoy simplifying my life and streamlining my business?

CHAPTER 7

Step 4: Goal-Free Zones and Goal Replacement Surgery

"Many people are climbing a ladder of success that's leaning against the wrong wall."

—STEPHEN COVEY

I recently attended a business conference with two hundred ridiculously high-achievers. These were the "alpha dogs" of business. I'd never been in a room with so many multi-millionaires. You would have recognized many of the attendees from their television appearances and other business ventures. Each of us paid $10,000 to attend, so the bar was pretty high just to get in the door.

Yet, even at this level of financial overachievement, I was shocked to see how often it came up that the people in the room were still holding themselves back from their full potential! For example, one entrepreneur I spoke with makes over $20 million dollars a year. He told me that when he started to make it really big, he also started to feel afraid, because nothing like this had ever happened to him (remember your Familiar Zone?). So he started to sabotage himself, but the most amazing part was *he could see it happening and still couldn't stop it.* He said it was like being in a train, and the train was going over the precipice, and he was helpless to prevent it. He told me that he lost about $170,000 in one week simply because he didn't know how to let himself succeed.

He finally said to me, "Too bad I didn't have your System then, because if I had done what you teach, I could have saved all that money!"

"SET YOUR GOALS"—UH, RIGHT

In traditional success programs, the very first thing they told us to do was "set your goals." This Step deals with that age-old question: "So how come I keep setting my goals . . . and keep not reaching them?"

As you've noticed by now, this System turns traditional success literature on its head. The reason we set goals and don't reach them doesn't mean we're not good enough, not smart enough, or not capable enough to get what we want. The reason we don't reach our goals is three-fold:

1. We're going after something we don't really want.

2. Our goals are impossible, outdated, or unrealistic.

3. We haven't given ourselves permission to *stop* setting goals.

Your Negative Reflection is always going to tell you that you're not good enough. Ironically, it's trying to protect you—because if you believe you're not good enough, then you won't try, so you won't fail. That's why the best way to overcome your Negative Reflection is to do the Steps of this System.

We know from physics that a body in motion tends to stay in motion. When a rocket ship leaves Earth, it must first overcome gravity, and secondly, break through the atmosphere. It's just like that with our lives.

Our *habits* are like gravity; that's what we're used to doing. We're used to thinking, "I can't do it," "I'm not good enough," and we're probably not used to asking for help, or accepting support from other people, or thinking there could be another way to live.

Our *environment* is like the atmosphere; that's where we exist. Being used to a certain environment is why even highly successful people may have to work at letting themselves succeed at higher and higher levels.

That's what this System is all about. You don't have to make any more expensive mistakes. Instead, learn from my mistakes and from the mistakes of others, and simply let yourself succeed.

GOAL-FREE ZONES

What is a **Goal-Free Zone**? A *Goal-Free Zone* is a time and place where you give yourself *permission to stop setting goals*. Why is this the next Step to enjoying more wealth and happiness?

1. To avoid burnout.

2. To get it that your worth doesn't come from your achievements.

3. To reduce the effects of Information Overload.

4. To reconnect with your Authentic Self.

Ironically, to be happy and rich, you need to give yourself permission to unplug from work. Scientific studies have found that human beings perform best in spurts of 90 to 120 minutes. Therefore, if you want to perform at your best, you must have times in your day when you unplug from work-related activities. You'll not only avoid burnout, you'll be better able to fully engage when you do go back to work.

The second reason to use Goal-Free Zones is because you need to understand that your worth does not come from your achievements. Many people subconsciously believe that they're only worthwhile when they achieve something or win awards or have lots of money. You need to truly realize that *your worth does not come from your achievements.* Your worth just *is.* To truly believe that, is the second reason to give yourself Goal-Free Zones.

The third reason you need Goal-Free Zones is to avoid the effects of Information Overload. While we can't stop the crush of information from email, cell phones, Crackberries, and every other electronic device known to man, we can at least limit it. The problem is, many people never unplug from all this noise, and the human organism was not designed to handle this kind of non-stop stimulus. That's one reason so many people feel stressed-out, burned out, in poor health, and have poor eating habits and a host of other health problems.

Fourth, when you do Goal-Free Zones, it allows you to reconnect with your Authentic Self; that still, small voice that is the voice of your intuition. Have you ever noticed that your best ideas do not come at work? They come when you're relaxing. They might come when you're jogging, journaling, praying, meditating, or in the shower. (That's what happened to me with Afformations!) Your mind is most receptive to ideas from the non-linear part of you at those relaxed times, and that's another reason to use Goal-Free Zones.

Oh, and the fifth reason? They're a lot more fun than working all the time.

If you keep your nose to the grindstone too long, eventually you'll have no nose.

EXERCISE: USING GOAL-FREE ZONES

1. What are my favorite Goal-Free Zone activities?
2. When do I enjoy doing them?
3. What negative beliefs do I have about doing Goal-Free Zones?
4. When are these beliefs not true?
5. What will happen if I don't use Goal-Free Zones?

Goal-Free Zone Questions 1 and 2—What are my favorite Goal-Free Zone activities and when do I enjoy doing them?

What do you like to do when you unplug from work? Maybe you enjoy meditating, journaling, walking, bicycling, jogging, exercising, or just napping. I would suggest not listing "watching TV" because I want you to be literally unplugged. When you watch TV, although it may be mindless, it's not truly rejuvenating. You usually don't feel refreshed after watching TV. Instead, you mostly feel dead, because you haven't engaged your mind and certainly haven't gotten in touch with Who You Really Are. TV is not designed to do that—its purpose is to get you to buy stuff!

Start by determining the activities you will do, and then plug in the different times for each of the different activities. You don't have to have fifteen different activities you do every day; that would defeat the purpose and just get you more stressed.

Just be sure you choose options that appeal to you. For example, my favorite Goal-Free Zone is napping. To write this book, for instance, I had a routine of writing for 90 minutes and then taking a 15-minute nap. Then, I'd come back to writing, feeling refreshed and ready to go.

Sometimes, I'd go for a walk and enjoy the sunshine—and suddenly, an idea would pop into my head. But usually those kind of creative ideas would not occur to me as I was sitting here writing. It took the active process of getting away from my writing to allow my creative intuition to kick in and let itself be heard.

You might only choose a few activities that you really enjoy, and that's all you need for your Goal-Free Zones. If you only do a few activities to rejuvenate and renew, as well as give yourself permission to unplug every 90 minutes, you will be ahead of all the people who are totally stressed out. We see health problems every day, such as obesity, stress, and burnout, and we just accept them as normal. They may be normal in today's society, but they're certainly not natural in terms of what makes us happy and successful. Remember, the purpose of this System is to help you be happy and rich!

The bottom line is: If you want to be rich, you cannot be normal. The people making millions every year are not normal—because by definition, normal equals not-very-successful. Is the majority of the population happy and rich? Nope. Therefore, if you want to be happy and rich, you must do things that "normal" people either don't or won't do.

The great news is, leaving "normal" means you don't have to do what most people do, which is spend most of their lives broke and miserable. If people give you a hard time, remember this great quote: *"I may be weird, but you're broke!"*

Goal-Free Zone Question 3—What negative beliefs do I have about doing Goal-Free Zones?

I can hear you now, *"I don't have the time, I don't have the money, I don't have the energy."* Sound familiar?

How about this one: *"I can't afford it."*

"I don't deserve it."

"My father taught me to work hard."

"My boss will never let me do this."

"I don't have any time because of the kids."
Whatever your beliefs are, write them down.

Goal-Free Zone Question 4—When are these beliefs not true?

When is it a lie that "I don't have the time"? Only every day! Everyone on Earth gets the same twenty-four hours each day. Even Warren Buffet can't stop the Earth's rotation, although I hear he and Bill are still working on that.

You make time for the things that are truly important, whether or not you're doing it consciously. But don't lie to yourself and say that you don't have the time. I can hear you saying, "But Noah, you don't understand. I'm busy doing a million other things. I've got all these other responsibilities." No kidding. That's exactly what we're talking about! I just want you to understand that when you say that you don't have time, you are lying to yourself.

Remember, what needs to get done, gets done. Do you recall our example of your best friend in the hospital? You got there, even though "go to hospital" wasn't on your to-do list.

The point is, when something becomes a *priority* for you, you find a way to make it happen. That is the ultimate expression of your Why-To's and Why-Not-To's: when something is important enough to you, you find a way, no matter what the cost.

What I'm doing here is exposing your Negative Reflection. You may say to me, "Noah, I don't have the time to do this." That, as we've just seen, is a lie.

But you could say to me, "Noah, I haven't made this a priority in my life." Now that statement is accurate. If you're not taking Goal-Free Zones, you have simply not made it a priority in your life yet. Once you realize that, you can start to live on the level of Conscious Choice, not Subconscious No-Choice.

What about the excuse of, "I don't have the money"? How much money does it take to meditate? To journal? To walk in nature? To get up from your computer? Do you have to pay somebody fifty bucks every time you meditate or get up? If so, I'm not sure where you're working, but you might want to check the medical plan.

How about reading a book? Go to the library. It's free. See, I can take away all of your excuses. You might not like me when I do this, because your Negative Reflection—which you think is you—is running out of excuses.

If nothing else, remember this:

**If you want to be happy and rich,
do what happy, rich people do.**

Either that, or you can sit there hoping a genie comes out of a bottle or a bag of gold falls from the sky. Let me know how that works out for you.

Goal-Free Zone Question 5—What will happen if I don't use Goal-Free Zones?

Remember your Why-To's and Why-Not-To's? Pain is a great motivator. If you realize that if you don't do Goal-Free Zones, you're going to experience a whole lot of pain—that may motivate you to do them.

If you keep doing what you're doing, you'll keep getting what you've been getting. My experience working with countless thousands at my seminars and mentorship programs has nailed into my cranium one simple and annoying fact: there are no shortcuts. This might rub some people the wrong way, but what I'm hoping to show you is that I truly want you to succeed.

If you came to this course telling me, "I want to be rich and happy," and you were currently broke and miserable, then I told you that you're doing fine and just keep doing what you're doing, I would be doing you a great disservice, wouldn't I? It would be like being overweight, hiring a personal trainer, having him come to your house, and when he got there, having him say, "Oh, you don't need to work out. You're fine."

Sure, *we'd like to hear that;* and we'd like to believe we don't have to change to get the things we want. But the truth is, we do need to do those sit-ups and those push-ups, if we want to get in physical shape. My job is to get you in fiscal, as well as physical, shape.

GAIN SUPPORT, DUMP EXCUSES

The next exercise is called "Gaining Support for Goal-Free Zones." People say, "Noah, I can't do this. You don't understand. I've got kids, my job, my boss who doesn't understand me." Yeah, I've only heard this about a million times.

So let's gain support and dump excuses. Below, I want you to list the individual Goal-Free Zone activities that you want to do, what you're saying is stopping you from doing them, who you need support from to do them, and what form you'd like that support to take.

Let's look at an example. Let's say you'd like to take more walks in nature. That's a Goal-Free Zone *activity*. What's stopping you? Perhaps, the belief that you don't have time. *"I've got the kids. I've got meals to cook. I've got a business to run. I've got a million other things I need to take care of."* Maybe you're saying, "Noah, you just don't understand my life." Fine. Write it down.

Who do you need support from, to actually do these Goal-Free Zones? If you're honest, you could say that you need support from your spouse to help you create more free time in your day. What about your kids? Maybe they can help with the laundry, cooking, cleaning, or other housework. You shouldn't be trying to do it all by yourself.

Maybe, if you don't have children or they are too young to help you, a housekeeper could come in twice a month or once a week to help. If you can't afford a housekeeper, maybe you could barter something with a friend. What if you started to think like a rich, happy person—what would they do?

EXERCISE: GAINING SUPPORT
FOR GOAL-FREE ZONES

GFZ Activity	What's Stopping Me From Doing It	Who I Need Support From	What Form I'd Like That Support to Take

You can pay a person with something other than money. Money is just one form of barter. Find something. Ask yourself: "What form do I need that support to take?" For the housekeeper example, you might need them to come in and clean or cook. Using a personal example, I needed help with administrative duties, which meant that I needed an assistant. I made the list of tasks, duties, and responsibilities I needed someone to do, then asked my friends who they knew who might be able to help me. I placed ads online and kept asking. Within a matter of days, a friend found the perfect assistant for me—but only because I kept asking and followed my own System.

HOW TO NOT CHANGE YOUR LIFE

I hate to be this obvious, but if you're telling me that you want to be rich and happy, then start doing what rich, happy people do. Rich, happy people are not any smarter than you. (Trust me. I've met lots of them.)

They're very average people, no more hardworking, or intelligent, or charming than anyone else. The essential difference between them and 97 percent of the world's population is that *rich, happy people have developed the skills of being rich and happy*. How's that for a major "duh"?

The fact remains that you can be rich and happy, too; but you can't sit there with your excuses, keep doing what you've always done and wonder why you're not rich and happy.

Most people are running harder and harder just to get the same results—or less. Happy, successful people know how to get the most out of every day because they have become experts at *managing* their sources of energy.

We have four sources of personal energy: **Physical, Emotional, Mental,** and **Spiritual.** Our Physical energy is our *quantity* of energy, or how much energy we have at any given time. Our Emotional energy is the *quality* of our energy, or how we express that energy in a given time period.

Our Mental energy means our ability to *focus* on a task for a period of time. And our Spiritual energy relates to our sense of being or *purpose* on Earth.

There are two things we can do with our personal energy: spend it and renew it. Most of us are great at spending our energy, and horrible at renewing it. Managing your sources of energy means letting yourself spend your energy wisely, and renew it consistently.

Over time, as you get better at renewing your sources of energy, you will increase your capacity to perform at higher and higher levels. Just like starting a new workout routine, what began as very difficult, even impossible, becomes easier and easier the more you practice.

After completing this exercise, if you find you're not very good at renewing your sources of energy, use Goal-Free Zones to renew your energy and refill your tank. It's pretty simple: rich, happy people use Goal-Free Zones. If you don't, your ability to succeed at higher levels will be very restricted.

EXERCISE: MANAGING YOUR SOURCES OF ENERGY

	Column A: *How I'm SPENDING My*	Column B: *How I'm RENEWING My*
PHYSICAL ENERGY: (Quantity)		
EMOTIONAL ENERGY: (Quality)		

	Column A: *How I'm SPENDING My*	Column B: *How I'm RENEWING My*
MENTAL ENERGY: (Focus)		
SPIRITUAL ENERGY: (Purpose)		

GOAL REPLACEMENT SURGERY: ARE YOUR GOALS REALLY YOURS?

Tim Taylor was a multi-millionaire real estate investor who had set a goal to retire by age 40. He beat his goal by a year, and retired at age 39. He moved to Florida and decided to spend a year relaxing on the world's greatest beaches. He began his vacation and had the time of his life—for 47 days.

On the 47th day, he was sitting on the beach in Cancun, Mexico, thinking about life, and he found himself wondering, "I have achieved the American Dream. I'm rich, successful, and retired at age 39. So why do I feel empty?"

He canceled the rest of his trips and went on a search for meaning in his life. A friend told Tim to attend one of my seminars. After taking my course and completing the Steps, Tim realized that even though he had made millions in real estate, he now wanted to do something else with his life. He wanted to be a real estate success coach, to share his knowledge to help others achieve their dreams.

Does Tim's story resonate with you? Do you want to do something with your life—but you're not quite sure what it is, or how to get there? Or maybe you've been going after something that you don't really want anymore. Or maybe you just need to understand why you're going after what you've been going after.

You may need to perform **Goal Replacement Surgery**.

PERFORMING GOAL REPLACEMENT SURGERY

What is Goal Replacement Surgery? When I discovered success anorexia, I realized that one of the hidden reasons so many people have their foot on the brake is that they're going after something they don't want anymore. Or, they're going after goals that aren't theirs. Or, they're going after goals that somebody told them they had to do, and inside, they don't want to do it.

Whatever the reason, their inner or outer circumstances have changed—but they're still on the treadmill, running after something they don't really want anymore. That's why sometimes, we have to perform Goal Replacement Surgery.

Three kinds of goals require Goal Replacement Surgery:

1. Impossible goals

2. Someone else's goals

3. Goals you don't really want anymore.

IMPOSSIBLE GOALS

What is an *impossible goal*? An impossible goal is just what it sounds like: a goal that can't be done. An example of an impossible goal might be *to make everyone happy*. You cannot make everyone happy. In fact, you can't technically *make* anyone happy. You can *influence* people's happiness; but you can't *make* anyone else happy.

How about this one: *"I have to be perfect and never make a mistake."* Yeah, that's the key to success, all right. Notice how perfect all the rich, happy people are. (Are you getting the humor here?)

How about this impossible goal: *"I have to sell 100 percent of my prospects."* Come on! I don't care if you're handing out $20 bills; there are people who wouldn't take what you're offering. (I wouldn't recommend this, unless, of course, you come over to my house.)

Now, you may say, "But I don't have any of those impossible goals, Noah!" Fine. Just realize that none of these impossible goals are conscious. No one wakes up in the morning and says, *"I have to make everyone happy today! If I don't sell 100 percent of my prospects, I'm not good enough! I have to be perfect today!"* No one does this . . . Consciously.

Impossible goals are not conscious; that is the very point. The reason we beat ourselves up for not reaching these impossible goals is because they lie in our Subconscious Mind, and that's what we're unknowingly reacting to.

That's why the purpose of Goal Replacement Surgery is to make that which has been subconscious, conscious—so you can examine your hidden, no-longer-valid goals and, if need be, let them go. Just like actual surgery on your physical body, you can't actually see what's going on inside of you—but if you're having a heart attack, might it not be a good idea to get in there and fix the problem?

SOMEONE ELSE'S/OUTDATED GOALS

The next set of incorrect goals is *someone else's goals*. For example, the guy who became a dentist because his father was a dentist, and his grandfather was a dentist, and he was expected to be a dentist. But he really wants to be an engineer. Or a clothing designer. Or an astronaut. Whatever it is, have you ingested goals from someone else that you don't really want?

The third set of goals that require Goal Replacement Surgery is *outdated goals you don't really want anymore*. Are you going after something you told yourself you had to do? For example, let's say you set a goal for yourself and you haven't achieved it yet. That's very common. But the question is: Do you still really want this goal, or have you just held on to it so long, you think you should still want it?

WHAT TIM DID

After I taught him Goal Replacement Surgery, Tim realized that he had been telling himself that he had to go back and build up his real estate investment company again, which he figured would take another three years and about three million dollars.

Once he did this Step, which took him about ten minutes, he asked himself, "Wait a minute. Why do I have to do that? Who's telling me that? Who made up that rule?" He realized that he was the only one who was saying he had to do it!

He then asked himself, "Why do I need to waste all that time, money, and effort doing something I don't even want to do—when I can just start being a real estate success coach like I really want to be?"

He realized that the truth was, he was afraid. He thought that by going back to what he'd always done, he wouldn't feel afraid anymore. But that was just fear holding him back from what he really wanted in the first place!

Once he realized what he'd been telling himself—and the fact that it wasn't true—he faced his fear head-on. In forty days, he packed everything he had, sold his business, moved from Florida to San Diego and launched his real estate coaching company.

Tim told me, "Noah, what you taught me in ten minutes saved me three million dollars and three years of my life. And in less than 180 days, I made more than $500,000 doing what I love."

Maybe you won't make a cool half mil or save three million bucks right away like Tim did. But, what if doing this Step helps you make an additional $1,000, or even $500 a month? Wouldn't that be a good return on your investment? This is what can happen when you do the Steps I'm showing you.

You might say, "Noah, I don't have any impossible goals, and I'm not going after something I don't want." Great! If that's true, then simply skip this Step. Most of the people I've worked with, however, have at least one goal they've been unknowingly going after, that needs to be replaced.

EXERCISE: PERFORM GOAL REPLACEMENT SURGERY

1. What are my current goals that need to be replaced?

2. Why do I have to do them and who told me I had to?

3. Why are they impossible goals, someone else's goals, or goals I don't really want anymore?

4. What PRINCIPLES do I choose to live by?

5. Why?

6. What ACTIONS can I do to replace my false goals with my True Principles?

I want to direct your attention to question 4—"What *principles* do I choose to live by?" Notice that I didn't ask you what your goals are. For this exercise, it doesn't matter what your goals are. I want to know what *principles* you choose to live by. Why? Because that's what's going to tell me Who You Really Are and whether or not you'll reach your goals.

In his seminal book, *The Seven Habits of Highly Effective People,* Stephen Covey writes about the nature of principles. He talks about the principles of *fairness, integrity, honesty, human dignity, service, excellence, potential,* and *growth.*

Principles are not processes. They are the fundamental guidelines for human conduct. He writes: "Principles are essentially unarguable, because they're self-evident. One way to quickly grasp the self-evident nature of principles is to simply consider the absurdity of attempting to live an effective life based on their opposites. I don't think anybody would seriously consider unfairness, deceit, uselessness, mediocrity or degeneration to be a solid foundation for lasting happiness."

What principles do you choose to live by? That's what I want to know about you. It doesn't really matter what your goals are. If you're saying, "My goal is to be a millionaire," but the principles you are living by are unfairness, laziness, and mediocrity, the odds of you accomplishing your goal are approximately that of a camel's chance in a supernova.

Once you have answered the question of what principles you choose to live by, you need to know why you are choosing that. That's question 5—Why? Because you're an adult. Nobody can tell you what to do or why. You make those decisions for yourself. As an adult, it's time to move from No Choice to Choice. So, answer the question for yourself.

YOUR ACTIONS REVEAL YOUR PRINCIPLES

The final question for performing Goal Replacement Surgery is, "What ACTIONS can I do to replace my false goals with my **True Principles**?" How are you going to demonstrate your True Principles? You can say that you live by honesty, integrity, service, quality, and excellence, but then sit around eating potato chips, watching TV, worrying all the time and telling yourself that you can't do it.

I'm not trying to pick on you. I'm trying to show you that you need to stop beating yourself up, stop beating your body up, and start showing the world that you live by these principles you say you do.

What if, by doing these Steps, you could save a year of your life? What about six months? How about a month? The point is you can't get those days back, since time is the one human resource that can never be replaced. Isn't it worth the ten or twenty minutes to have the opportunity to possibly save years of your life and who knows how much money?

This is one of the Steps that rich, happy people have already done, whether or not they know it. They're not perfect, but they're almost always going after what they really want, not what someone else thinks they should want. That's where I want you to be, too.

A QUICK RECAP

1. We've been inundated with "set your goals" information over the past fifty years. Yet, many people remain stuck, either because they feel guilt-tripped every time they stop, or they're going after goals they don't really want.

2. To dramatically increase your productivity, use **Goal-Free Zones**, which are times in your day when you give yourself permission take a break from goal-related activities. Superstar athletes and business high achievers understand the importance of relaxing, renewing, and recharging.

3. Don't feel guilty when you take a Goal-Free Zone. But don't stress about it, either. Allow yourself a 10 to 15 minute break every 90 minutes. Scientific studies have shown that the human organism functions best when breaks are taken every 90 minutes.

4. Goal Replacement Surgery means asking the question: "Are my goals really mine?" Many people are going after goals that they either don't want anymore, or weren't theirs to begin with.

5. If you identify impossible goals, someone else's goals, or outdated goals that you've been going after, simply release them—and give yourself permission to go after what you really want.

Next Actions: List three things you can do from this chapter in the next seven days to use Goal-Free Zones and perform Goal Replacement Surgery in your life and business.

1._____

2._____

3._____

TOP 10 AFFORMATIONS FOR STEP 4:

1. Why do I love using Goal-Free Zones?

2. Why do I have permission to unplug?

3. Why am I allowed to relax and renew every day?

4. Why do I take responsibility for renewing my energy?

5. Why do I get support in renewing my energy?

6. Why do I love going after what I really want?

7. Why do I have permission to be Who I Really Am?

8. Why am I allowed to be, do, and have what I really want in life?

9. Why do I take full responsibility for living my dreams?

10. Why am I allowed to be Who I Really Am and succeed?

CHAPTER 8

Step 5: Who Are You Trying to Protect, Punish, or Please?

"Heat not a furnace for your foe
so hot that it do singe yourself."

—WILLIAM SHAKESPEARE

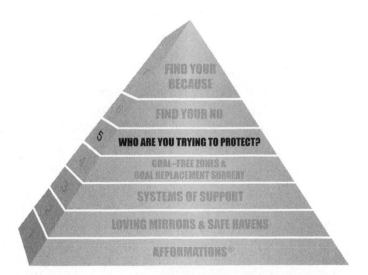

Barbara had spent tens of thousands of dollars and years of her life trying to become more successful. She was smart, funny, motivated, and was now working in a direct selling company that gave great how-to training programs. Having worked for nearly ten years as an on-air personality, she certainly wasn't shy about talking with people. Yet, for some reason, she simply couldn't reach the level of success she knew she was capable of.

WHO ARE YOU TRYING TO PROTECT?

Perhaps the most hidden, subconscious reason we hold ourselves back from success is that *we are unknowingly trying to protect someone else from our own success.* I know that that is one of the strangest sentences in this book. Nevertheless, this phenomenon affects millions of men and women, nearly all of them without their conscious awareness.

For example, when I asked Barbara this question: "Who are you trying to protect from you being more successful?", it dawned on her that *she was holding herself back from success to protect her husband.* She realized, for the first time, that she was afraid that if she became the truly successful person that she knew she could be, his ego might be bruised. And what if he didn't love her anymore? What if he left her?

See how all those hidden fears added up to one whopper of a Why-Not-To?

Naturally, as Barbara was unknowingly holding herself back, she had no idea why she was doing it. That's why trying to protect someone from your success is one of the toughest Why-Not-To's to spot.

Barbara's fears went something like this: "What if I succeed and my husband's jealous of me? What if he doesn't appreciate what I do? What if I become too successful, and he leaves me?" Again, she didn't know she was thinking these thoughts; she hadn't recognized her own head trash. Yet there it was, holding her back from success in an attempt to protect her husband; and in the end, protect *herself* from the pain of abandonment.

EXERCISE: WHO ARE YOU TRYING TO PROTECT?

Who I'm Trying to Protect	Why	How It's Helped Me

Look at the three columns above. First, "Who am I trying to protect?" In Barbara's example, *"I'm trying to protect my husband from my being more successful than he is."*

The second column is, simply, "Why?" Why are you doing that? Barbara's answer: *"Because I'm afraid he'll be jealous of me and leave me if I'm more successful than him."*

Finally, list how trying to protect that person has helped you. Barbara's answer sounded something like this: *"I don't have to fear my husband's being jealous of me if I'm not successful. If I don't succeed, then what does he have to be jealous of? So I'll keep myself down, so that I protect myself and him."*

I know that seems totally counterintuitive and not logical, but just like Mr. Spock pointed out in *Star Trek*, what made you think humans are logical?

You may also be trying to protect your family from your success. The subconscious thinking goes something like this:

"Noah, what if I'm too successful, and I have to be away from my kids? What if I start to succeed really big, and I have to be on the road all the time? I could miss my kids' soccer games, ballet recitals, and, ultimately, miss my children growing up."

I can understand why you would feel that way; and when you put it that way, doesn't it make perfect sense why you'd hold yourself back? So, how has holding yourself back helped you?

The answer: If you're not too successful, you can be there for your family all the time.

Look, I'm not telling you what success is. I'm not saying that if you're not a millionaire, then you're not successful. That's none of my business, and it's nobody else's business either. That's your choice.

I don't care what kind of car you drive, where you live, how big your house is, or how much money you make. I mean that in a very loving way.

My point is, I want you to be the one deciding—not your Negative Reflection! Once you have your foot off the brake, and you're driving in the direction you really want to go, that's when you have permission to be and do whatever you—not your head trash—choose. That's a massive, fundamental distinction that you can now make for yourself.

WHO ARE YOU TRYING TO PUNISH?

Now, this is weird. Why would we try to *punish* someone by *holding ourselves back* from success? Let me give you an example.

Back in my twenties, when I was living in Hollywood, I remember one day realizing that I was angry with my parents for not supporting me in the way I thought they should have. On that day, I also realized that I had spent years unwittingly trying to punish them!

To help you understand this, here's how the "logic" went in my head: *"I'm mad at my parents because they didn't do what I wanted them to. So I'm going to punish them by not succeeding, so they can't point to me and say what a good job they did as parents. Ha! I'll show them!"*

What benefit did I get from this? Simple. I got to hold onto my anger and never step out of my Familiar Zone. (In case you are wondering whether I was a happy, successful person in those days . . . uh . . . yeah, right!)

I want you to write this sentence in big letters and put it on your desk:

THE POWER OF "I'LL SHOW YOU"

Never underestimate The power of "I'll Show You." Those three little words have driven more people to *fail* than anything else in the world. Ironically, those same three little words have also driven more people to *succeed* than anything else in the world. Why? Because: *"They said I couldn't do it. Oh yeah? I'll show you!"*

For instance, Mary Kay Ash was told by nearly everyone that she couldn't do it. As a woman in 1963 wanting to open a cosmetics company, her accountant and her attorney told her she was nuts. People around her told her she'd lose everything. To top it all off, just days before the company's opening, her husband died suddenly and unexpectedly. However, Mary Kay was driven by three powerful words: I'll Show You. With her company today bringing in more than $5 billion in revenues, I think she showed them.

You can think of dozens of successful people that this phrase has driven to succeed when everyone else said it couldn't be done. When somebody says, "You'll never be able to do that," it can either discourage you or drive you to succeed. Maybe people laughed at you when you sat down to play the piano, or hit a baseball, or start your own business . . . and maybe that gave you the attitude of, "I'll Show You."

Now you can use the power of "I'll Show You" to your advantage. Don't use it to beat yourself up or hold yourself back. Use it to let yourself succeed. Never underestimate the power of "I'll Show You"!

EXERCISE: WHO ARE YOU TRYING TO PUNISH?

Who I'm Trying to Punish	Why	How It's Hurt Them

WHO ARE YOU TRYING TO PLEASE?

Now let's look at the third subconscious reason people hold themselves back—the subconscious need to please others by either succeeding or not succeeding. This is the only question for which you can either succeed *or not succeed* by trying to please others. With the other two questions, you're trying to protect or punish yourself or others by stopping yourself from success. With this question, however, you may be trying to please others by either succeeding, or not letting yourself succeed.

For example, many of my Students who became very rich, but very unhappy, told me that they worked very hard to succeed so they could get approval from someone else, usually a parent. On the other hand, other Students have *stopped themselves* from succeeding to try to please someone else.

The real question in either case is: What are you really afraid of? If you're really honest with yourself, you might find that you're really afraid of *disapproval from others,* or of *not looking good* to the outside world.

People can say whatever they want, and they usually do. The question is: Why do you let that affect you? Is it because you're afraid of someone's disapproval?

If you're blaming others by saying, "So-and-so did this to me," then you're being a victim and have no power to change—and that's not acceptable. You have that power, and it's time to claim it.

EXERCISE: WHO ARE YOU TRYING TO PLEASE?

Who I'm Trying to Please	Why	What I'm Really Afraid Of

HOW TO RELEASE ANY FEAR

Do you know what *fear* really is?

Fear is NOT "False Evidence Appearing Real."
Fear is an emotion caused by *the expectation of pain*.

I know you were expecting me to say that old cliché. The fact is, some clever speaker came up with that acronym years ago, and it's become so popular that people think it's true. But that's not what fear is.

Fear is a very real human emotion that occurs when you anticipate or expect that something may hurt you. If you fear something, you are saying to you, "Hey! What if I get hurt by this?" Ironically, the emotion of fear is there to protect you; but it can also hold you back from growing.

We experience the feeling of fear when *we perceive that we're not in control.* Fear is the emotional effect of absence of personal control over your situation. Therefore, there's an inverse relationship between control and fear. The more control we have over our situation, the less fear we feel.

If we really want to conquer fear, we need a tool that enables us to gain, maintain, and protect our personal control. That's another reason we invented the Freedom Power Pack, because it gives you three Personal Control Strategies:

1. Maintenance Strategies to *maintain* control.
2. Enhancement Strategies to *improve* control.
3. Contingency Strategies to *regain* control if we lose it.

You can learn more about how to get your own Freedom Power Pack in the Additional Resources section at the back of this book.

How can you release fear? One great way to overcome fear is to *accept the pain that you might feel as a result of your actions.* So what if that person disapproves of you? Are you going to die? As far as we know, no one has ever died from disapproval.

Sure, you might feel some pain when someone disapproves of you—big deal. News flash: You're already in pain anyway! So you might as well go ahead and try whatever you're afraid of. You might just find that the words of Ralph Waldo Emerson were eminently true: "Inside of us, we all know that on the other side of fear lies freedom."

A QUICK RECAP

1. Many people are unknowingly holding themselves back from success because they're trying to protect, punish, or please someone else.

2. To stop doing this, first ask yourself, "Who am I trying to **protect** by being less than I am?"

3. Then, ask yourself, "Who am I trying to **punish** by holding myself back from success?"

4. Finally, ask yourself, "Who am I trying to **please** by succeeding or not succeeding?"

5. Stop trying to protect, punish, or please others with your success by realizing the payoff you've received from your behavior, and then give yourself permission to be as successful as you like.

Next Actions: List three things you can do in the next seven days to stop trying to protect, punish, or please others regarding your success.

1._____

2._____

3._____

TOP 10 AFFORMATIONS FOR STEP 5:

1. Why did I stop protecting others from my success?

2. Why did I stop punishing others by not succeeding?

3. Why did I stop trying to please people by not succeeding?

4. Why did I stop trying to please people by holding myself back?

5. Why am I allowed to be, do, and have exactly what I want on Earth?

6. Why am I so happy?

7. Why do I no longer fear being truly happy and really rich?

8. Why do I give myself permission to be as successful as I really want?

9. Why do I love being the truly successful person I've always wanted to be?

10. Why am I good enough, just the way I am?

CHAPTER 9

Step 6: Find Your No

**"There are many roads to success, but
only one sure road to failure; and that
is to try to please everyone else."**

—BENJAMIN FRANKLIN

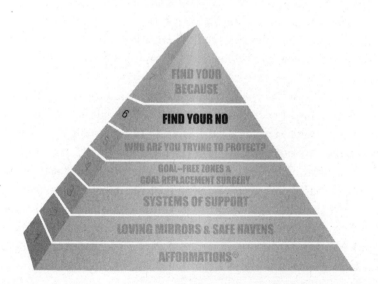

Do you ever feel guilty saying no to others? When people make
requests of you, do you treat the requests like orders to be obeyed?
Many people have lost their No—their ability to say no and not
feel guilty for it. We are socialized to be nice and make accommo-

dations for others. This is correct, because society wouldn't function very well if people just did whatever they wanted all the time.

However, some people have gone overboard and simply can't say no! Three Percenters, on the other hand, understand the importance of sticking to your agenda when other people's agendas diverge from your own.

Happy, successful people have learned how to disagree without being disagreeable. When you can say no with a smile, you will have mastered one of the most important Steps of *The Secret Code of Success*.

FIND YOUR NO

We're now at Step 6, which is **Find Your No**. Because so many people have lost their No, it's essential to find it again. Now, I could just say to you: "Okay, it's important to say no. Got it?" But it's much more complex than that. Traditional success teachers may have talked about the importance of saying no; but they haven't shown us *how to do it.*

In working with tens of thousands of Students at my seminars and mentorship programs, I've realized that saying no is not as easy as it sounds. If it were, there wouldn't be so many doormats or people-pleasers out there!

After working with thousands of people who had lost their No, I realized that there are three distinct aspects to Find Your No that you must master if you want to stop being a people-pleaser and start living the life you were meant to. You must **Find Your Personal No**, **Find Your Interpersonal No**, and **Find Your Global No**. Let's go through each of them in order . . .

FIND YOUR PERSONAL NO

While we know that many people have trouble saying no to others, has it ever occurred to you that you may have trouble saying no to *yourself?* In an earlier chapter, we talked about the fact that the only three resources we have on Earth are time, energy, and money. Well, what if you're doing things that waste your precious human resources? Are you going to get where you want to go? Maybe, but it will sure take longer than it has to.

To *Find Your Personal No* you examine the activities you're doing, and determine which ones are draining your time, money, or energy that you've allowed to continue. We looked at your Activities System in Step 3—but have you actually installed this System properly yet?

EXERCISE: FIND YOUR PERSONAL NO

1. Time-, Money-, or Energy-Draining Activities I'm doing: (Examples: procrastinating, smoking, worrying, overeating, etc.)

2. Why I'm doing them, and what it's COSTING me:

3. BETTER USES of my Resources of Time, Money, & Energy:

4. ACTIONS I can take to reallocate my Resources to get what I really want:

Be honest. Are you procrastinating? Smoking? Overeating? Under-eating? Binge spending? Spending too much time on the Internet or on email?

When I ask people in my seminars how many have a problem procrastinating, about 80 percent of the hands go up. Why do we procrastinate and why is it so costly to your success? Procrastination is, plain and simple, caused by fear. The fear of what? It depends. You might be afraid of not getting what you want, and you may be afraid of *getting* what you want!

Once you've listed what you're doing that's draining your time, money, or energy, I want you to take a close look and ask yourself, "Why am I doing these things, and what is it costing me?"

For example, why do you procrastinate? The only answer is fear, but fear of what? Do you have a fear of disapproval? Fear of failure? Fear of success? Do you have a fear of people not liking you, a fear of rejection? Do you find yourself asking, "What if this doesn't work out?" or even, "What if I become *too* successful?"

Throughout this book, I've shown you that we stop ourselves from success because we're afraid to get out of our Familiar Zone. There's nothing wrong with being afraid, but you do need to ask yourself the next part of the question: *What is that costing me?*

To say that it's costing you hundreds of thousands of dollars is probably very realistic. If you don't value your own time, money, or energy, the cost over your lifetime may be staggering. What if you smoke? *"I smoke because I'm addicted to it."* If that's the case, what's causing that addiction? And, what is that costing you?

Maybe you're addicted to caffeine or chocolate. I want you to get very honest with yourself. I'm not saying that you can't enjoy a cup of coffee or a bar of chocolate. I am saying, however, that many people are a mochafrappelattechino-a-day away from being a millionaire. Each of these silly drinks costs like five bucks. Do you really need that?

If you really want to gain leverage on yourself, add up how much you spend on coffee, or eating out, or binge spending over the course of a year, five years, ten years. I'm not trying to tell you how to live your life. I'm just inviting you to ask yourself, "Is this activity a money-helper or money-drainer? An energy-helper or energy-drainer? A time-helper or time-drainer?"

The next question is, "What are better uses of my resources of time, money, and energy?" Ask yourself, "Can I take that money that I'm spending on my $5-a-day, $25-a-week, $1,300-a-year drink, and do something more productive with it?" The fact is, *you know what you need to do.* You just don't want to admit that you know.

You might think, "That's nothing, Noah," but you could pay off a credit card with that kind of money. You could make an extra payment on your mortgage. You have the resources you have. The question is how can you use them better?

What are better uses of your resources of time, money, and energy? Everyone says, "I'll do _____ when I have more time, money, and energy." But you're not even using what you have now correctly!

USING WHAT YOU HAVE (CORRECTLY)

You have X money, X time, and X energy, and you're sitting around wishing you had Y and Z. But how are you supposed to get to Y and Z when you're not even taking care of X?

Whether or not you believe it, you are the one who decides where, how, and why your money is spent. Money doesn't walk around and say, "Hey, I think I'll spend myself over here." You are the one taking out that credit card. You're the one taking out that cash. Money can't think for itself. You're the thinker. So let's start thinking, and then start acting properly. That's where we go with the next question: "What ACTIONS can I take to reallocate my resources to get what I really want?"

Notice that I'm not telling you to make a million dollars, and then you'll be rich and happy. No, it doesn't happen that way. I know this is going to be one of the most obvious things that I could say, because frankly, when I first heard this truth, it was so stupidly obvious that I completely missed it. But here it is anyway:

Rich people are great at managing their money.

I know that's a massive, "Duh!" but sometimes what's obvious is what we miss. When I first heard that, I was like, "Yeah, whatever." Then, I said, "Wait, time out. Look at that statement, Noah. You're not doing the things that multi-millionaires do. So how do you expect to become one of them?"

Then I realized, "You're telling yourself that you're a victim here, and that you don't have any choice. But you do have a choice. I need to learn to manage my money like rich people do." That's when I started hanging out with mega-rich people who were also happy and fun, and my whole view of money and how to manage it began to change.

I'm not going to get into money management. That's not what this course is about. Plenty of people talk about money management, and I recommend that you do your homework on that topic. My point is that you need to understand that *you* are in charge of your money; money is not running you. *You* are the one who signs the check. *You* take out the credit card; it can't leap out of your wallet on its own. These are your ACTIONS, and your beliefs lead to those ACTIONS.

REALLOCATING YOUR RESOURCES

So when you look at the question above: "What ACTIONS can I take to reallocate my resources of time, money, and energy?", list what you can do differently, that rich, happy people are doing to manage their resources. If you don't know the answer to that, start hanging out with rich, happy people and see for yourself what they do.

No matter how bad things seem to be, you can always find someone in your community or your network who is doing well. Contact her and say, "Mary, I've noticed that you're really good with money, and I really admire you. I want to make some changes in my life, and I was wondering if I could ask for your advice. Could you sit down with me and look at my budget? I don't know where all of my money is going. Can you help me?"

What's the worst thing Mary can say? Right: "No." And then

you're no worse off than you were before! But if you Ask from a place of genuine Acknowledgement (remember your first 2 A's of your People System?), Mary just might say yes.

Do you see how all the Steps of this System work together? That's why this is a System and not a bunch of ideas just thrown together. Remember, the Three Percenters are doing this, whether or not they know it. And if you're looking for a more advanced productivity tool to help you leverage all of your available resources to achieve better results, see the new Freedom Power Pack in the Additional Resources section at the back of this book. Now let's go to the next aspect of Find Your No . . .

FIND YOUR INTERPERSONAL NO

The first step was a no from you to you. Now, you're saying no to others. This is where you will *Find Your Interpersonal No.* When people make demands of you that you simply can't or don't want to do, you have the power to say no. One thing I've taught thousands of people in my seminars is to use the three-step **Detect, Deflect, and Reflect Method** to Find Your Interpersonal No.

EXERCISE: FIND YOUR INTERPERSONAL NO

Detect (I see the demand)	Deflect (I ask what's behind it)	Reflect (I synergize)

I broke this Step down into its essential components because I used to be a doormat—a people-pleasing, nice guy with very low self-esteem. And since I had no self-esteem, I tried to get everyone to like me. Problem was, as good ol' Ben Franklin said, "There are many roads to success, but only one sure road to failure—and that is to try to please everyone else." Since that was what I was doing, I was on the sure road to failure . . . come to think of it, I had pretty much arrived.

In creating *The Secret Code of Success*, I realized, "Wait a minute. If you look at rich, happy people, they don't have a problem saying no. Imagine how many people are asking Bill Gates for something every day. The richer and more successful you get, the more demands are placed upon you. So you can't be truly happy and rich without being able to say no."

At that point in my life, I wasn't even aware of all the ways I was saying yes when I really wanted to say no. That's when I realized the first step to say no to others is to simply *become aware that someone is asking you to do something, and that you can either say no or yes to that request.*

I'm sure that sounds ridiculously obvious to those of you who don't have a problem saying no. For the rest of us, it may be the biggest awareness of our lives. Like Pavlov's dog, when someone asked me to do something, I would just do it without thinking. They ask; I do. They ask; I do. There were no thoughts behind my actions. It was a *reaction*, rather than a *response*.

DETECT—BECOMING AWARE

So, the first step is to *Detect*, "Hey, someone is asking me to do something here." The next step is to *Deflect*. What does that mean? The basic idea is to break down their request into exactly what they want. "What are they asking me to do?"

Picture somebody standing in front of you asking you to do something. Now that you can Detect it, you see the request coming at you, kind of like an arrow. Then, you Deflect that arrow. So imagine that arrow making a U-turn. It doesn't hit you, but it turns around right in front of you and goes back to them.

DEFLECT THE ARROW

You can Deflect by asking that person, "What exactly do you mean by that? Tell me more about that. Why do you want that? Help me understand what you're looking for." You become like Detective Columbo—the TV character who solved every mystery by asking lots of "dumb" questions that other people were too cool to ask. Now you can be "uncool" and ask the questions that no one else is asking. I make a great living asking "dumb" questions!

Once you've turned that arrow around in the Deflect step, the final step in the trilogy is to *Reflect*. That's when you send the arrow right back to them and *synergize*. You get beneath their request and find what's really going on.

You might say, "I would love to do what you're asking, but I'm not going to be able to give it the attention that it deserves. So I'm going to have to decline right now. However, I do know someone who may be able to help you . . ."

THE SYNERGY STEP

When you say no when you mean no, you're actually doing that other person a favor—because you not only protected your time, you also protected your relationship. Have you ever said yes when you meant no, and ended up *resenting the other person*? You're nodding your head, aren't you?

When you say no in a way that protects the other person's pride, but also protects your time, you also protect the relationship. You can even be as blatantly obvious as that: "Bob, if I say yes to that, I'm going to end up resenting you, and our relationship is far too important for that. That's why I'm going to have to say no."

If your time is the most valuable commodity you have, shouldn't you protect it with your life? Remember that committee you really didn't want to be on, or that event you agreed to go to, that you really didn't want to attend? You're nodding again, aren't you?

Of course, there are many times in life when you simply can't say no—for example, to your boss or when you're expected to do things in your job. The point, however, is when you Find Your No, you might also find that you can begin the transition from doing things that Empty Your Tank to more of the things that Fill Your Tank.

The essential point here is that if you don't value your time, nobody else will. Have you ever noticed that there are certain people in your life whom you have learned not to ask for things, because they almost always say no? They've Found Their No big time. You can learn a lot from someone like this. I'm not suggesting you should become a selfish jerk; but the fact remains, you can learn a lot from a jerk!

TEN KEY PHRASES FOR FINDING YOUR INTERPERSONAL NO

The Three Percenters understand the importance of saying no even when other people are demanding a yes. Often simply having the correct phrases at your fingertips can help, because then you don't have to make something up on the spot. Use these key phrases as a starting point for Finding Your Interpersonal No:

1. I'd love to help, but I'm cutting back on the time I spend in that area.

2. How about we talk about this next year?

3. I like to schedule in those types of requests several days ahead; can you make that work for you?

4. I can hear the urgency about this, but I'm just not set up to respond to emergencies.

5. That sounds like so much fun! But it's not just for me.

6. Why are you pushing me so hard?

7. I understand there are consequences when I say no to this, but I'm willing to live with those consequences.

8. You've been so good to me, but I need to say no to this. Is there something else I can do?

9. That's just not the sort of thing I can respond to in this life-time.

10. I would love to chat, but this is part of my business day and I'm focused on earning money. How about tonight?

The ability to disagree without being disagreeable is a learned skill that's simple on the far side of complexity. It would be simplistic to say, "Just say no." That's simple on the *near* side of complexity, whereas simple on the *far* side of complexity means to take these steps, yet keep it simple. I've broken it down for you so you can realize, "Wow, I didn't even realize how much I was saying yes when I meant no. Now I can take the steps to Find My No with myself and others, too."

Which brings us to the final aspect of Find Your No . . .

FIND YOUR GLOBAL NO

Okay, we've covered your Personal No and your Interpersonal No. Now, it's time to *Find Your Global No*. Your Global No means you know your purpose on Earth, and you commit to stay on track, even when it's easy and tempting to get off track.

When you know your **Ultimate Yes**—your purpose or mission (which we'll cover in the next, final Step), it's much easier to say no to what's not truly important and what doesn't fit in with your mission. Your Global No deals with one fundamental issue, that of *integrity*.

ACTING WITH INTEGRITY

When you act with integrity, you are who you say you are, and you simply don't deviate from that. The problem is, in our modern society, it's very easy to deviate and try to take shortcuts. Does the word *Enron* mean anything to you? You can open up any newspaper and see stories about how people and companies tried to take shortcuts in the name of making more profits. The point, however, is that people run companies; companies don't run themselves.

There are always shortcuts. There are always things that will make you think, "Hmmm, I could do this and nobody will find out." The funny thing is, sooner or later, the hens come home to roost. If you deviate from integrity, someone will find out eventually. Believe me, I'm speaking from painful experience.

SAYING NO NO-NO'S

When I worked as a temp in Los Angeles, they sent me on assignments as a secretary for big movie studios. Because I didn't have much money, I would often take things like office supplies, pens, and the like. Basically, whatever fit in my duffel bag was fair game. I figured, "Hey, these guys are rich and I'm broke; who's going to miss it? And I *deserve* to take this, because I'm working so hard for so little." I actually convinced myself that I *deserved* this stuff I wasn't paying for!

But then a funny thing started to happen over and over. The pattern was always the same: My bosses would love me because I was such a good worker. They would try to get me hired as a full-time employee. But time after time, something would happen and I'd never get the job. Someone else with fewer qualifications would get the job and I'd be back out there, shuffling from one temp job to another.

I can remember one time I worked in one particular office for nearly six months—that's a long temp assignment! I became friends with the people in the department, and they said, "Oh, you're definitely going to get this job!" Naturally, when the time came to make it a permanent position, they gave it to someone else.

After many, *many* experiences like this, I started to wonder what the hell was going on. "How come, if I'm so good," I asked myself, "I never get the job?" About this time, I started my studies of Universal Law and how your thoughts create your life. I had never realized how my thoughts, beliefs, and actions were creating my life; I thought I was a victim and that God just had it in for me.

One day, I realized by stealing little things, I was telling God, "I don't have money, so I have to steal from others." My actions were saying, "I don't have." And God reflected back, "Okay, you don't have." As I was *taking from others*, so I was *taken from*.

COMING FROM "I HAVE"

The next day, the phone rang—my temp service, offering me a new position at the most prestigious movie studio in town. I showed up and they showed me to my cubicle and desk. Then, my boss showed me to the Holy Land—the office supply cabinet! But this was no ordinary office supply cabinet; when the doors opened, I actually heard angels singing. Approximately the size of Montana, it was filled with every office supply you could think of. I think it was actually the original Staples location.

Okay, maybe I'm exaggerating a little, but you get the idea. The point is, she literally said, and I swear I'm not making this up, "Help yourself to whatever you need." Whatever I need?! I'm going to need a bigger duffel bag!

As I stood there salivating, I remembered what I had finally realized. "If you keep coming from 'I don't have', you're going to keep *not having*. Is that what you really want for your life, Noah?"

As my boss walked away, leaving me before the gates of office supply heaven, my hands, shaking, slowly shut the doors. And I never took anything from that office supply cabinet—not even a paper clip.

Now, you might think this is a pretty silly story and a nutty example of how not to live your life. But after that incident, I began, for the first time, to really ask what I wanted to do with my life. And I realized that I wanted to teach people and write books . . . even though I had no idea what to talk about. Five years later, I discovered success anorexia, and that led to the work I'm doing now: helping countless thousands of people through seminars and mentorship programs.

The point is, if I had stayed with my old thinking and behavior of "I don't have," do you think any of what I'm doing now would have happened? Me neither. So, be careful what you say and do—because that will become your very life.

EXERCISE: FINDING YOUR GLOBAL NO

1. What are my Why-To's of acting with integrity?

2. What will I GAIN if I act with integrity and purpose?

3. What will I LOSE if I act with integrity and purpose?

4. People I admire and why (their aspects of character I'd like to adopt):

In the exercise above, I've given you four simple questions to Find Your Global No. First, *"What are my Why-To's of acting with integrity?"* Why do you want to do this? Understand, living from your Global No means you're not going to steal or lie; you're going to act with integrity, and you're going to stand your ground, even if it's unpopular. Why would you want to do that? You need to figure it out.

Question 2, *"What will I GAIN if I act with integrity and purpose?"* You won't do it if you don't gain from it, right? Therefore, what are you going to gain? The clearer you are on what you gain, the easier it will be to act.

Question 3: *"What will I LOSE if I act with integrity and purpose?"* Did you realize that, if you act with integrity and purpose, you will lose something? For example, you'll lose the ability to steal from people, to rip people off, and lie to them. Bummer, huh?

That's why I'm very careful about what I say. My word means a lot to me, and the people around me know that my word means a lot. I don't make a lot of promises, but when I do make a promise, it's going to happen—usually before I say it will. Unsuccessful, unhappy people do the reverse: They make tons of promises with lots of talk and no action. How's that working out?

THE INTEGRITY QUESTION

You have to communicate your intentions of integrity to your team. You have to talk the walk, as well as walk the talk. For example, I recently had a production meeting with my team, and I communicated my vision both verbally and in writing to them. I told them, "This is where we're going. We are here to change the world. Are you with me or not? Let's go."

My enthusiasm rubbed off, and they became excited about it, too. So they said, "Let's do it!" My team got it because I was very clear in saying, "I'm doing this. I'd love to do it with you guys, but if you're not on board, tell me now, because I only want to work with people who are with me 100 percent."

I wanted to be absolutely sure that every person on my team was on board with my vision. Guess what? They all signed up.

On a scale of 1 to 10, all talk and no action would be like some-one who is an 8 with talk and a 2 with action. Don't be that person. Be an 8 with talk and a 10 with action. You do need to communicate your vision in words, but you also need action to back it up.

Finally, list *people you admire and why.* List their aspects of char-acter that you would like to adopt. What would Stephen Covey do? What would Jack Canfield do? That's what I often ask myself. In your business, look at who you admire, and ask, "What would this person who I respect, do?' You might ask, "What would my leader do? What would my upline do?" Look at the people you respect and admire, and ask, What would they do? This is how you can begin to think like them. Choose your mentors wisely, because you become who you follow.

A QUICK RECAP

1. One of the most important things you can do to get your foot off the brake is **Find Your No.** That's because highly success-ful, happy people have given themselves permission to say no when they mean no.

2. The three aspects to Find Your No are: Find Your Personal No, Find Your Interpersonal No, and Find Your Global No.

3. Find Your Personal No means saying no to yourself. Un-successful, unhappy people have a hard time saying no to things they know aren't good for them, or don't produce the results they want. Identify the actions you're doing that are taking you away from what you really want, then become accountable to others to stop doing them.

4. Find Your Interpersonal No means saying no to others. Rich, happy people know how to say no when other people's de-mands don't fit into their own vision for success. Learn to say no with a smile.

5. Find Your Global No means your integrity—the things you are not willing to do that would compromise your principles. When you come from "I don't have," the universe has no choice but to reflect back, "Okay, you don't have." Instead, come from "I have"—and God will respond with a life of true abundance.

Next Actions: List three things you can do from this chapter in the next seven days to Find Your No for greater peace of mind and satisfaction in your life and business.

1._____

2._____

3._____

TOP 10 AFFORMATIONS FOR STEP 6:

1. Why is it easy for me to say no when I mean no?

2. Why do I love saying no with a smile?

3. Why do I enjoy synergizing?

4. Why do I love finding better solutions for myself and others?

5. Why do people look at me as a leader?

6. Why am I comfortable in my own skin?

7. Why do I have all that I need?

8. Why do I have more than enough to be all that I want?

9. Why am I so confident?

10. Why am I enough?

CHAPTER 10

Step 7: Find Your Because

"This is the true joy in life: the being used for a
purpose recognized by yourself as a mighty one."

—GEORGE BERNARD SHAW

When we look at the Three Percenters—happy, successful people
who are the Naturals of Success—we finally realize that they are
being who they are and living their purpose in life. Whether working, relaxing, or playing, this means you stop apologizing for being
and expressing Who You Really Are, and allow yourself to prosper
for that expression.

Most people don't know why they're here on Earth. That leads to feelings ranging from depression, frustration, and stress to rage, guilt, and despair. To **Find Your Because** means you know your Ultimate Why-To, which ultimately is *to be and express Who You Really Are, and allow yourself to prosper as you serve others.* When you Find Your Because, you will have taken the most important step to become *fundamentally unstoppable*—because a person who acts on purpose may be slowed, but they can never be stopped.

People don't follow followers. People follow leaders.

You can be that leader—but to do that, you must Find Your Because. The three aspects to Find Your Because are:

1. **Define Your Core Competencies**

2. **Identify Your Avenues of Expression**

3. **Release Your Spirit**

DEFINE YOUR CORE COMPETENCIES

Your *Core Competencies* are simply what you're naturally good at. Having worked with tens of thousands of people in my seminars, I've realized that to Define Your Core Competencies means to combine your Strengths, Skills, and Desires.

Core Competencies Part 1—Describe Your Strengths

There's been a lot of talk about Strengths recently. Essentially, a *Strength* is something you do naturally, something you love doing, and something that makes you feel good after you've done it. Here are four fill-in-the-blank questions to identify your natural Strengths.

Describe Your Strengths

1. I feel strong when:
2. People I trust have told me my Strengths are:
3. Specific ACTIONS the following leaders do/did that I admire:
4. ACTIONS I can do to express my Strengths:

Core Competencies Part 2—Document Your Skills

Your Strengths and your Skills are different. A Strength is something you do naturally, while a *Skill* is an activity you do that reveals that Strength. For example, let's say you're a great communicator. You can convince anybody to do anything. That's a natural Strength. Then, your Skills could be in selling, recruiting, teaching, or broadcasting.

Let's say you're a natural analyzer; you see how things fit together. Your Skills could be in money management, engineering, or medicine. Your natural Strengths lead to your expressed Skills.

Document Your Skills

1. I know I'm really good at:
2. People tell me they appreciate it or like it when I:
3. I love doing:
4. ACTIONS I can do to increase my skills:

Core Competencies Part 3—Define Your Desires

What can you do to follow your dreams? What ACTIONS could you take that would help you fulfill your Desires? See how we're always taking ACTION on every little Step?

Don't wait until you know every single thing before you start moving. That would be like wanting to take a trip and waiting for every light to be green before you leave. Most people live their lives that way, waiting for things to be perfect before they'll act. The Three Percenters realize that life ain't perfect, and simply *act*. You can do this, too.

Define Your Desires

1. If money were no object, I would:
2. I'm happiest when I:
3. I'm excited when:
4. ACTIONS I can do to follow my dreams:

IDENTIFY YOUR AVENUES OF EXPRESSION

The second aspect of Finding Your Because is to Identify Your Avenues of Expression. This is how you're going to express your Strengths, Skills, and Desires. You first need to Define Your Core Competencies; then, determine how you would like to express them in your life. *"This is what I really want to do. This is how I want to express Who I Really Am."*

Avenues of Expression
Part 1–Reveal Who You Really Are

This goes all the way back to Step 1. You can ask your Loving Mirrors and Safe Havens to help you answer this question. *"Who am I?"* may be the oldest question known to humanity. See if you can bring the answer for you into a word or a phrase. Reach inside and express Who You Really Are.

Who I Really Am:

_____

_____

_____

Avenues of Expression Part 2—Review Your Roles

Once you have revealed who you are, you need to Review Your Roles. These are roles you currently do, as well as those you would like to do. Your roles are not the same as your job. Your roles are everything your job entails, and more. For example, you might have the role of mother or father, brother or sister, spouse and friend—those are all personal roles. Then, you might also have the role of a salesperson, recruiter, coach, or mentor—all of these roles may be encompassed by your job.

What about roles you'd like to do, for those dreams you would like to fulfill? If you start doing the things that happy, successful people do, you will become one of them. By the same token, if you don't do what they do, you will not become one of them.

That doesn't mean you have to do it exactly the same way someone else did it. I've interviewed hundreds of super-successful people, and no two got there the same way. But they're all doing one thing the same: expressing who they are to a very high degree, and letting themselves prosper for that. If they can do it, you can do it, too.

Key Roles I Do and Would Like to Do:

_____

_____

_____

Avenues of Expression Part 3—Resolve to Persist

This is your Ultimate Why-To. Why will you Resolve to Persist? When you start moving up, stuff gets thrown at you that you could never anticipate. It's happened to me, it's happened to others, and it will happen to you. But when you Resolve to Persist, you become *fundamentally unstoppable.* That's when you move beyond positive thinking, beyond motivation, and just get stuff done.

My purpose here on Earth is to create a nation and a world of Loving Mirrors. I do that through my seminars, through mentoring and training, and through living my life. That's my Ultimate Why-To.

What's yours? You may not know consciously yet; but you need to find out. Why? Because if you don't, at the first red light you come to—and there will be lots of them—without a strong enough Why-To, you'll give up and go home. Will you give up, or will you keep moving in the direction of your dreams? If you turn around and go home, I guess you didn't want it that bad.

The key is to know when you have too many red lights in a particular direction. Maybe you do need to take another path. The more you are in touch with your intuition, your Authentic Self, the more you will know when you need to keep going in that direction, and when to take a different way. There are plenty of paths to Success. Ask yourself why you'll never stop until you get there.

Why I Will Persist (My Ultimate Why-To):

_____

_____

_____

RELEASE YOUR SPIRIT

The final aspect of the final Step is to Release Your Spirit. If I could sum up the essence of the entire *Secret Code of Success* teaching, it would be in those three simple words: *Release Your Spirit.* There are only three things you need to do to Release Your Spirit; but before I tell you what they are, I want to tell you something that may surprise you.

THE TWO SENTENCES THAT DESCRIBE
ALL HUMAN EMOTION

I was meditating one morning when I realized that all human emotion can be described in two simple sentences. Once I saw them in my mind, I realized that they encompassed the entire range of human emotion—and they made it so simple, they also encompassed how to "fix" any negative emotion we might experience for the rest of our lives.

Ready? Here are the sentences:

When your opinion of your past, present, and future tends to be positive, you will be happy.

When your opinion of your past, present, or future tends to be negative, you will be unhappy.

Those two sentences describe all human emotion. What is the key word in both of those sentences? *Opinion.* Why? Because it's not what happens to us, it's our *opinion* of what happens to us, that determines our thoughts, feelings, actions, and responses—and all of those together create our very lives.

How many people do you know who are carrying around a negative opinion of something that happened to them ten, twenty, forty years in the *past*, that's determining their lives today? How many people do you know who are not appreciating the abundance they have in the *present*, right under their noses? How many people do you know who are afraid of what's going to happen in the *future*?

Conversely, how many people do you know who have a *positive opinion* of their past, present and future? Notice that your past, present, and future ARE your life. You can very easily make the argument that *your life is nothing more than your opinion of your past, present, and future.*

Where is your past? Where does it exist? Only in your head. Nowhere else in the entire universe but your head. I don't care if you have twelve brothers and sisters; not one of them is carrying around your past.

Where is *your present*? Only in your head. No one on Earth is experiencing your present.

Where is *your future*? Same as the other two—it only exists in your head.

Therefore, if you get only one thing from this book, I hope you get this, because this simple thought may be the greatest gift of this entire teaching:

> **If you want to Release Your Spirit and live the life of your dreams, all you have to do is change your opinion of your past, present, and future.**

And how do we do that? It's as easy as 1–2–3.

THE THREE STAGES TO RELEASE YOUR SPIRIT

Stage 1: Forgive Your Past

Stage 2: Appreciate Your Present

Stage 3: Step Into Your Best Future

Release Your Spirit Stage 1-Forgive Your Past

The only thing we need to do with the past is to *forgive* it. The past is gone, but you may be holding on to it.

> **When you do not forgive your past, you are bound to the past by chains that are stronger than steel.**

I know you don't want to be chained to the past; but in order to not be, you have to forgive it.

A lot of people have big problems with this. The truth is, you are forgiving for yourself, not the other person. Look at the word *forgive*. It means to "give-for." You are *giving for* the purpose of being free. You are forgiving for you, not for them. We're not condoning what was done to us, and we're not saying it's all right. No, it wasn't all right. It sucked—but it's gone.

As masters over the centuries have told us, "Let the dead bury the dead." It's not our job to go back and refight what's gone forever. When you try to do that, you're just chained there forever.

In the spaces below, write who you need to forgive, for what, and your Why-To's of forgiving now. Notice I didn't ask you how to forgive. My experience with thousands of Students shows that when you have the Why-To's of forgiving, the heart finds the How.

EXERCISE: FORGIVE YOUR PAST

Who I Need to Forgive	For What	My Why-To's of Forgiving

Release Your Spirit Stage 2—Appreciate Your Present

Stage 2 of Release Your Spirit is to Appreciate Your Present. The word *appreciate* literally means "to raise in value." What are most people doing? Right: the exact opposite. They're *depreciating* what they have. "Why don't I have what they have? Why don't I have as much money as them? Blah blah blah . . ."

Yes, it's good to have goals and to strive for them. But the problem comes when nothing is ever good enough for you. I'm inviting you to look at what you have and simply appreciate it. I'm not saying that if you're $30,000 in debt, you should try to deny that and say everything's wonderful.

You might say, "Noah, I'm in big financial trouble right now. I've got bills, I've got debt, and I'm not making much money. But I'm still breathing. I've got all my fingers and toes. My eyes work. My ears work. I can type and I can talk. I've got a phone and I've got a computer. I've got a brain that works."

You may think this is silly. But I'm not being facetious here. Do you have any idea how many people have none of the things you take for granted every day? You enjoy all this bounty and abundance without thinking, and almost certainly without appreciation.

Do you remember what happened on September 11, 2001? Remember the aftermath of Hurricane Katrina? Do you know what happened in your mind, after the horror of seeing those pictures on TV? The first thing that happened in your mind, whether or not you realized it, was that you automatically focused on everything you HAVE. You watched so many people lose so much— their homes, their friends, their very lives—and somewhere inside of you, you said to yourself, *"Thank God I have so much."*

After September 11th, I remember watching along with everyone else as the Twin Towers crumbled to the ground. I was living in Massachusetts at the time, and I turned off the TV, got in my car, drove to my parents' home in Maine, and hugged them. Why did I do this? I guess it was some sort of instinct that told me to hold onto and appreciate everything I had been blessed with.

I hope I'm jarring you a little bit, because we just don't realize what a miracle life is. Sadly, it often takes a tragedy to show us everything we already have. That's where the phrase, "You don't know what you've got 'til it's gone" comes from.

But here's a little secret—actually, it's a huge secret:

You don't have to wait until something's taken from you in order to appreciate the fact that it's there.

In the exercise below, I want you to list what you like about your present. I hope you take a lot more room than this page to do that! Then, I want you to write what you *don't* like about your present situation. *"I don't like that I'm $20,000 in debt. I don't like that I'm not making enough money to be able to take more vacations. I don't like where I'm living . . ."* Whatever it is. Be honest. Give yourself permission to tell the truth without judging yourself. And no, you do not have to share this list with anyone.

Look: You're already thinking this stuff in your head. I'm just asking you to write it down! The main reason positive thinking doesn't really work is because there's always stuff you don't like about your life. Why lie about it or try to pretend it's not there?

In the third column, I want you to answer: "Who can help me grow?" The reason I didn't ask you, "How can I change?" is because if you knew how to change, you'd already be doing it! Answering the question, "Who can help me grow?" focuses your mind on the resources you can find. These can be in the form of books, CDs, seminars, coaching, mentoring, or friends. You have resources right under your nose that you've allowed to depreciate. Now, it's time to appreciate them—so you don't have to lose them.

EXERCISE: APPRECIATE YOUR PRESENT

What I Like About My Present	What I Don't Like	Who Can Help Me Grow

Release Your Spirit Stage 3—Step Into Your Best Future

The final stage to Release Your Spirit is to *Step Into Your Best Future*. We've all done exercises where we've written about our ideal future and tried to imagine what it would be like to live there. But I'd like you to do something different this time.

Here's something strange that the gurus never told us about Success: We live our lives in days. I know that sounds obvious; but the gurus have told us to write about how wonderful everything will be, some time in the future, when everything's perfect.

Well, I hate to say this, but life on Earth ain't perfect. Many of my closest friends are multi-millionaires, and not one of their lives is perfect. So, rather than trying to envision some glorious, idealized future where everything's perfect, I want you to try something that is, ironically, a whole lot easier.

In the space below or in your *Secret Code of Success Journal,* I want you to write what happens in Your Perfect Average Day. I learned this exercise from Frank Kern, one of my brilliant mentors who happens to live a life most of us can only dream of. He spends most of his days surfing off the coast of San Diego while his online businesses rake in over a million dollars a *month.* Yes, a month—not year. Frank says that he did this exercise when he was making good money but was pretty miserable, because he hated what he was doing and who he was doing it with.

In less than a year after doing this exercise, his life completely changed from having lots of money and being miserable, to having even more money and being ridiculously happy.

I want you to think about your average day that you live right now. What happens in your average day? You wake up. You open your eyes. Maybe the alarm clock goes off, because you don't really want to get up and do what you're doing. (Note: I haven't needed to use an alarm clock for over twenty years. Think that may have something to do with the fact that I love what I do and do what I love?)

You get out of bed. You eat breakfast—or not. Maybe the kids are running around, getting ready for school. You go to work. Are you doing something you love? Do you work out of your home? Do you go into an office?

You go through your day. Are you happy? Bored? Excited? Feeling a sense of significance and contribution?

You come home. Are you tired? Worn out? Exhausted? Exhilarated? Happy? Satisfied?

You go to bed. What are the last thoughts you think before drifting off to sleep? Contentment? Thanksgiving? Dread at the thought of having to do it all over again tomorrow?

Do you see what I'm getting at? This is how you live your life. And before you know it, a year's gone by . . . two years . . . five years . . . ten years . . . twenty years . . . and more. And you're still saying to yourself, "Someday I'll . . ."

Have you ever noticed that there are no trips to Someday Isle? We either start doing the thing, or it never happens. So I'm inviting you to stop thinking about Someday Isle . . . and just start doing the damn thing.

In your *Secret Code of Success Journal,* write what happens in Your Perfect Average Day. The key word there is *Average.* I don't want you to write about some idealized future where you're sitting on the beach sipping margaritas every day—because I've talked with many people who've done just that, and believe it or not, it actually does get boring after a while.

Yes, we want to enjoy vacations and nice stuff; but this exercise is about *describing what happens in a perfect average day when you are happy and doing what you really want.*

EXERCISE: STEP INTO YOUR BEST FUTURE

My Perfect Average Day:

To *Release Your Spirit* represents the highest level of success, happiness, and fulfillment, because you finally stop worrying about money or making people happy. You simply express Who You Really Are and let yourself prosper as you prosper others. The Three Percenters may be unconscious of what they're doing, but you can still learn from them. This final aspect of the final Step means you have not only stopped apologizing for Who You Are, but you give yourself *permission to* succeed at the highest levels.

The wonderful thing is, as you give yourself *permission to succeed,* you also give others that same permission. That's why to Release Your Spirit represents the culmination of this work and brings us full circle—back to the gaining and giving of the unconditional support we all need to be Who We Really Are.

A QUICK RECAP

1. The final Step of *The Secret Code of Success* is to **Find Your Because**. This represents your Ultimate Why-To; your purpose or mission. When you Find Your Because and start living it, you become *fundamentally unstoppable.*

2. The first aspect of Find Your Because is to **Define Your Core Competencies**. This happens in three stages: *Describe Your Strengths, Document Your Skills,* and *Define Your Desires.*

3. The second aspect of Find Your Because is to **Identify Your Avenues of Expression**. The three stages are: *Reveal Who You Really Are, Review Your Roles,* and *Resolve to Persist.*

4. The third and final aspect of Find Your Because is to **Release Your Spirit**. The three stages to Release Your Spirit are: *Forgive Your Past, Appreciate Your Present,* and *Step Into Your Best Future.*

5. To Find Your Because represents the highest achievement a human being can do, because the greatest joy comes from giving yourself to a purpose larger than yourself. Use these Steps to Find

Your Because—because when you give yourself permission to be Who You Really Are, you give others that permission, too.

Next Actions: List three things you can do from this chapter in the next seven days to Find Your Because in your life and business.

1._____

2._____

3._____

TOP 10 AFFORMATIONS FOR STEP 7:

1. Why did I Find My Because?

2. Why am I living a purpose-driven life?

3. Why do I know why I'm here on Earth?

4. Why did I find my Ultimate Why-To?

5. Why is it so easy for me to focus on what I really want?

6. Why am I on course and on target?

7. Why did I never, ever, ever give up?

8. Why is everything going according to plan?

9. Why does God bless me with unprecedented favor today?

10. Why am I fundamentally unstoppable?

ACT III

NEXT STEPS

CHAPTER 11

Now What?

> "I have learned this: If one advances confidently
> in the direction of his dreams, and endeavors to
> live the life which he has imagined, he will meet
> with success unexpected in common hours."
>
> —HENRY DAVID THOREAU

The quote above has three verbs—*advances, endeavors* and *meet.*
First, you advance, which means you progress. The word *progress*
comes from the Latin word *progredi,* which means "to step forward." You don't have to jump off a cliff as some have suggested;
you simply need to take one step at a time.

Notice how you'll be advancing: confidently. Why? Because
you're working with Universal Law, which is law that can't be
broken. You don't have to think, "I can do it"; instead, think: "We
can do it." *We* can do a lot more than *you.*

Now, where are you advancing confidently? *In the direction of
your dreams.* You don't have to know the exact end point—just
the direction. You don't have to know exactly how you're going to
get there; that's another reason to take one step at a time. If you

follow the Steps, take one step at a time, and *endeavor* to live the life you've imagined, what happens next?

You will *meet* with Success. I just love that, because *meeting* Success implies that Success is waiting for you, like you're going on a date. When do you meet someone? When they're *expecting* you, when they're anticipating getting together. Why don't you picture Success as someone waiting for you, just as excitedly as you can't wait to get together with them?

YOU, MEET SUCCESS

Remember, the Three Stages of Self-Belief are:

- First, other people believe in you.
- Second, you believe in others.
- Third, you believe in you.

This book was written to help you become happily successful in your life, career, and relationships.

But what do you do now that the book is over? If you really want the results and benefits you desire for your life—things like more money, greater wealth, better relationships, or a closer connection with God—you must do what I shared with you in Chapter 3: *Take ACTION!*

In this book, I've introduced you to *The Secret Code of Success*: The fastest, simplest, and most effective way I've ever seen to get your foot off the brake and let yourself be truly wealthy and happy. I showed you how to get rid of your head trash and create the life you've always wanted.

You've learned the seven Steps that, if you do them, will change your life. I urge you to do the exercises in each chapter and use your new, empowering Afformations. Do these simple Steps daily, because doing this will turn these new behaviors into new habits, and your new habits will become your new life.

If you want to create a rich, happy life, then you must, by definition, move into a new Familiar Zone. That means you must *practice the Steps*. Not just read about them, talk about them, or think about them . . . but actually do them!

Right now, your Negative Reflection may be telling you things like, *"I can't do it . . . it's too hard . . . I don't have time."* As I showed you, your Negative Reflection's job is to keep you right where you are, in your current Familiar Zone.

If you want to move into a new Familiar Zone (that is, being happy and rich), simply follow this three-step process:

1. Learn.

2. Do.

3. Teach.

To *Learn* means to learn the Steps of *The Secret Code of Success*. I've just given them to you. The Three Percenters—the Naturals of Success—unconsciously do these Steps in essentially every area of their lives, careers, and relationships. They usually don't know that they're doing it, which is why they have trouble teaching it. Nevertheless, if you pay attention, you can learn a lot from a person acting unconsciously.

Second, you must *Do* the Steps. The only exercise program that doesn't work is the one you don't use. But the hardest part of any exercise program is to get off the couch and do it. The great news is, getting support to do these Steps is contained right in the System. You don't have to do this alone—and in fact, that's the very point of *The Secret Code of Success*.

Finally, to get the full Benefit of what I've shared with you, you must *Teach* it to others. You must share what you've learned in this book with the people in your personal and professional life—your friends and family as well as your team members and business colleagues.

Who learns more, the teacher or the student? We've all experienced having to teach something to a group or even one other person—and that's when you truly learn.

Also, consider the people on your team, in your organization, or in your social circle. How many of them would you say are holding themselves back to some degree, whether in business or in life? That would be, what—all?

If that's true, don't you owe it to them to share this information? If you are their friend, and if you care about them at all, don't you want to see them become the whole, complete person they were meant to be? Wouldn't you want a friend to do the same for you?

If you don't feel comfortable with the word *teach*, use the word *share*. If you found something you know could help improve the lives of those around you, wouldn't you naturally share it with them? That's what I'm encouraging you to do—not only for their benefit, but for *your* Benefit, as well.

I also have several free gifts that will make this even easier for you. Go to **www.SecretCodeBook.com/iafform** for your FREE **iAfform Afformations® Stress-Buster Session**. *iAfform* Sessions are spoken Afformations set to inspiring music, that you can listen to anywhere, anytime throughout your day to help you embrace your new, empowering thought patterns.

As you listen to your iAfform Audios, your subconscious thought patterns are rewired from negative to positive—and you're able to manifest whatever you want TWICE as fast with HALF the effort!

iAfform Audios are available to help you:

- Make more money
- Lose weight
- Find love
- End stress
- Sleep better

Go to **www.SecretCodeBook.com/iafform** for your FREE 60-Second Stress-Buster Session.

Also, see the Free Bonus Gift at the back of this book for another truly special experience that can transform your results very quickly.

I also suggest you reread this book from start to finish at least two more times, underlining and highlighting the passages with particular meaning to you. "What?" your Negative Reflection is saying. "I just finished the book, why do I have to read it over and over again?" The fact is, the more you study this book, the faster you will start to live The Code—and the faster and easier your wealth and happiness will manifest.

After I discovered success anorexia, I realized it was my duty and responsibility to bring this teaching to the tens of millions of people around the world who, through no fault of their own, are starving themselves of success. My mission is to create a nation and a world of Loving Mirrors, and to assist those with the same vision on the way to true wealth, peace, and joy.

I am privileged to lead seminars, workshops, and mentorship programs that transform people's lives quickly and permanently. That's why I want to personally invite you to join me at my *Success Camp 2.0 Weekend Seminar.*

This event will take you to an entirely new level of success, because we actually change your relationship to Success right on the spot. I will show you exactly how to break through whatever is holding you back from reaching your full potential. You will walk out of the program with tools, skills, and strategies that will give you a new way to walk through life, attract more money, enjoy more fulfilling relationships, and be at peace with yourself.

Many of my Students count *Success Camp 2.0* as a turning point in their lives. It's exciting, fun, and packed with real-world skills to become truly wealthy in every sense of the word. You'll also meet like-minded people from all over the world, many of whom could become business associates and lifelong friends.

This course is so essential for you to attend that, for a limited time, I have decided to provide a scholarship for you and a family member to attend the course free as our guests. That's right, both of you come *free*!

See the following pages for more details about this valuable offer to you.

I look forward to being a part of your Success Story!

All the best,

NOAH ST. JOHN

CHAPTER 12

Your Free Bonus Gift

Noah St. John's
Success Camp 2.0 FREE!

As a thank-you for purchasing *The Secret Code of Success*, Noah St. John is offering a scholarship for you and a guest to attend his *Success Camp 2.0* as his complimentary guests. That is a total value of $2,990—for free!

These guest seats are available to purchasers of Noah St. John's *The Secret Code of Success* published by Collins. The course must be completed by July 1, 2010, and this offer is made on a space-available basis. All seating is first come, first served. To assure your spot, please register immediately at **www.SecretCodeBook.com**

At Noah's **Success Camp 2.0** live seminar, you will build on what you learned in this book by discovering:

✔ Why you're going down the road of life with one foot on the brake

✔ *The Secret Code of Success* that the top 3 percent know—that they're not even consciously aware of

✔ What "motivational" speakers don't want you to know

✔ How Noah's students have doubled, tripled, even quintupled their income in less than a year—and how you can, too
✔ How to truly get your foot off the brake in your life, career, and relationships
✔ How to stop going after what you don't want and let yourself get what you really want
✔ The #1 secret to success that almost everyone ignores
✔ The inner game of time management to remove procrastination once and for all
✔ How to release your hidden emotional blocks to being truly wealthy in all aspects of life

By the end of the course, you will release your inner hidden blocks to true wealth and success. Best of all, the same strategies that work to create material success work to enhance your relationships, health, and happiness as well.

No matter your current level of wealth—millionaire, middle-class, or broke—if you're not totally satisfied with your income, your net worth, or your level of happiness, and you want to finally feel what it's like to go down the road of life without your foot on the brake, then register for Noah's Success Camp 2.0 seminar today because . . .

Isn't it time you stopped living with one foot on the brake?

Register now at www.SecretCodeBook.com

"Noah's work represents one of the most significant breakthroughs in the study of success in decades. If you want to eliminate the fear of success and live the life you've imagined, you owe it to yourself to attend his programs."
—Jack Canfield, author of *Chicken Soup for the Soul*® and star of *The Secret*

"Noah St. John's Secret Code of Success *is discovering within ourselves what we should have known all along—we are truly powerful beings with unlimited potential."*
—Stephen R. Covey, author of *The 7 Habits of Highly Effective People*

"Using humor and down-to-earth language, Noah gives you a step-by-step method to live the life you want and deserve."
—John Gray, Ph.D., author of *Men Are From Mars, Women Are From Venus* and star of *The Secret*

"You'll never get your foot off the brake and achieve the success you desire unless you take Noah's advice to heart."
—T. Harv Eker, author of *Secrets of the Millionaire Mind*

SUCCESS CAMP 2.0 CERTIFICATE

Noah St. John and The Success
Clinic invite you and one
friend to attend Noah's
Success Camp 2.0 Seminar,
as complimentary guests.

To register and for more
information, go to:

www.SecretCodeBook.com

If you have no access to a computer, call
our 24-hour Free Recording at:

1-800-392-9883 ext. 9000*

* The offer is open to all purchasers of *The Secret Code of Success*™ by Noah St. John. Original proof of purchase is required. The offer is limited to the Success Camp 2.0 seminar only, and your registration for the seminar is subject to availability of space and/or changes to program schedule. Corporate or organizational purchasers may not use one book to invite more than two people. The Success Clinic reserves the right to refuse admission to anyone it believes may disrupt the seminar, and to remove from the premises anyone it believes is disrupting the seminar. While participants will be responsible for their travel and other costs, admission to the program is complimentary. Participants in the seminars are under no additional financial obligation whatsoever to The Success Clinic or Noah St. John. The course must be completed by July 31, 2010. The value of this free admission for you and a companion is $2,990 as of February 2009.

CHAPTER 13

Spread the Word

The three Steps to Success:
1. Find something that improves people's lives.
2. Tell everyone about it.
3. Repeat.

—NOAH ST. JOHN

Okay, so now you know the Steps to get your foot off the brake for good. The only question now is are you going to share what you've learned or keep it to yourself?

As I've shared with tens of thousands of people, the only things you have to do to succeed in life are: *Learn, Do,* and *Teach.*

First, *Learn* what it takes to succeed. That's what this book and my other courses and programs are all about. Second, *Do* the Steps. It's one thing to know, and quite another to take what you know and put it into ACTION. But taking action is the only way to manifest the wealth and happiness you desire.

And finally, *Teach* what you've learned to others. The best way we can learn ourselves is when we share what we've learned with others.

Because this is true, I encourage you to share what you've experienced in this book with others. Get the message of this book out to as many people as possible. Commit to telling at least one hundred of your friends, family, and associates about it or consider getting it for them as a life-changing gift.

Not only will you be introducing them to a new (and easier) way of thinking that can change their lives, they will also learn a new way of being in this world that will uplift everyone who gets this message.

What are you waiting for?

FACT: YOU CAN DOUBLE YOUR INCOME WHILE WORKING LESS THAN YOU ARE RIGHT NOW. HERE'S HOW.

It's true: The Three Percenters are working less than you are right now. *A lot less.* They don't have any more hours in the day than you do. They aren't any smarter than you are. But they're getting much more from everything they've got.

YOU CAN EASILY DO WHAT HAPPY, RICH PEOPLE DO

In my Home Study Course: "**The Secret Code of Success™: How to Double Your Income in 90 Days and Let Yourself Enjoy It!**" you'll learn how to:

- **Explode your daily productivity**
- Take calculated risks with total confidence of success
- **Decide what you really, really want—then let yourself get it!**
- Eliminate procrastination once and for all
- **Remove the clutter from your life and your office**

- Stop working so hard to get what you really want
- **Stop trying to reach your goals through sheer willpower (it's one of the least effective things you can do)**
- Double your income while taking more time off

YOU ALSO GET *FOUR* ADDITIONAL BONUSES

- **The Complete Course Transcripts**—Easy-to-follow for faster learning
- **The Complete Action Guides**—Your step-by-step guide
- **Executive Summaries for Each Module**—Checklists to keep you on track
- **The Complete Coaching Calls**—I walk you through life and business challenges

Over $500,000 from ONE idea . . .
"I made over $500,000 from just ONE idea Noah gave me in 10 minutes. If you're serious about wanting to live the life you want, working with Noah is the best decision you'll ever make!"
—**Tim Taylor,** Real Estate Success Coach

Over $1 Million in Sales . . .
"Dear Noah, Your program enabled me to stop feeling anxious and directionless regarding my future sales funnel. I'm now at well <u>over one million dollars</u> in sales thanks to your Course. Thank you!"
—**Kim Toomey,** Pennsylvania

My Home Study Course is delivered right to your computer. No shipping, no waiting, no hassle!

To order, visit:
www.SecretCodeBook.com/homestudy
Enter this coupon code: **code3** for special *Surprise* Bonuses!

IT'S TRUE: PEOPLE WITH BETTER TOOLS ACHIEVE UP TO 80% MORE EVERY DAY. NOW IT'S <u>YOUR</u> TURN.

Finally . . . a planner that puts you IN control, not UNDER control.

Most people are going down the road of life with one foot on the brake and one on the gas. The problem is, most so-called "productivity" tools just tell you to step on the GAS harder: *"Set your goals! Work harder!"* But how far are you going to get with your foot still on the BRAKE?

In humans, "Foot-On-The-Brake Syndrome" occurs when we can't decide which demands on our time and attention should have priority. If we choose to do *this*, then we can't be doing *that*, and if we do *that*, then what about all of *those*?

So we end up jammed in the middle of a growing pile of clamoring demands and rapidly mounting stress, until we're practically incapable of doing anything meaningful or fulfilling.

Sound familiar?

It's time to break free and seize control of your own life— quickly and simply!

From $5,000 to $75,000 a month in 160 days . . .
"I went from $5,000 to $75,000 in monthly sales in less than 160 days as a result of working with Noah. Thank you for taking the lid off my thinking and letting me know I could have the BEST!"
—Sheila Valles, California

The Freedom PowerPack™ helps you decide WHAT to do and WHY, then HOW to do it for the best results in the shortest time. And because it's modular, with full integration, you can create your own solution to suit your own unique needs. The Freedom PowerPack™ is fully compatible with *The Secret Code of*

Success™ and *Afformations*®. It will also turbo-charge any other planner you're currently using—even your electronic PDA!

Learn more—and create your *personal* Freedom PowerPack™—at
www.SecretCodeBook.com/freedom

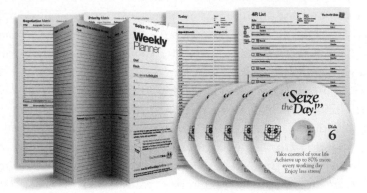

FACT: NOAH CAN SHOW YOUR ORGANIZATION HOW TO GET BETTER RESULTS WITH LESS TIME, MONEY, AND EFFORT.

Keynotes and Workshops

The Secret Code of Success™: "How to Stop Living with One Foot on the Brake!" *(Sales/Motivation/Peak Performance)*
- A little assumption that's costing you a fortune
- Why motivational programs so often fail (HINT: It's not what they're teaching, it's what they're *not* teaching that matters)
- The #1 secret of success that almost everyone's ignoring
- How to get your organization's foot off the brake . . . *and much more*

Lose the WAIT™: "The E.A.S.Y. Way to Eliminate Procrastination and Explode Productivity" *(Leadership/Time Management/Productivity)*
- The top five productivity killers and how to avoid them
- How to make better, quicker decisions
- Three easy ways to cut meeting times by 25 percent
- The E.A.S.Y. Way to explode your productivity . . . *and much more*

Do Less, Have More™: "What Every Busy Person Should Know about Work-Life Balance" *(Productivity/Work-Life Balance)*
- The antidote to the "too much to do, too little time" syndrome
- How traditional teachers told you to handle the pressure— and why the solution is often worse than the original problem
- How to de-clutter your home and work environment with one simple technique
- The amazingly simple technique that boosts your daily productivity . . . *and much more*

ADDITIONAL PROGRAMS TO GET YOU BETTER, FASTER RESULTS

- Secret Code Train the Trainer™ Programs
- Live Tele-Trainings and Webinars/Distance Learning
- C-Level and Management Coaching and Mentorship
- Quantity Discounts on *The Secret Code of Success* book

Call 1–800–392–9883 ext. 9001 or visit **SuccessClinic.com** for more information.

ACKNOWLEDGMENTS

My Most Grateful Thanks:

To Jack Canfield, who believed in the message of this book when it was a bunch of pages bound with a piece of tape.

To Janet Switzer, who saw the potential in this teaching and sent one email that changed my life.

To Stephen Hanselman of LevelFiveMedia, who understood my entire teaching with one phone call. This man gets it.

To my editor Hollis Heimbouch, whose insights made this book zing.

To Steve Ross and everyone on the Collins team who got on board for the ride, including Doug Jones, Larry Hughes, Angie Lee, Kimberly Crowser, Ben Steinberg, and everyone else behind the scenes.

To my Director of Marketing Projects, Donna Friedman, who constantly amazes me.

To the mentors, teachers and coaches who've guided me, including Alex Mandossian, Frank Kern, Eben Pagan, Scott Martineau, John Counsel, Neale Donald Walsch, Joe Vitale, Harv Eker, Anthony Robbins, Roy H. Williams, Harvey Mackay, Jim Collins, and Michael Nitti.

To Josh Cantwell of Strategic Real Estate Coach and Greg Clement of RealeFlow, for shaving years off my learning curve and introducing my work to your wonderful students worldwide.

To Dan Hollings, the marketing mastermind for *The Secret*, for teaching me how to reach more people through BridgeGAP Marketing.

To Heather Kirk and Megan Johnson, for creating artwork that proves that a picture is indeed worth 1,000 words.

To Gary Vaynerchuk of WineLibraryTV, who taught me how to create a community of millions while we drove around in my car in Cleveland, Ohio.

To Stephen Covey, who inspired me to get into this business when a recording of *The Seven Habits of Highly Effective People* fell off a bookshelf and hit me on the head. I'm serious. It's hard, even for me, to ignore a sign like that.

To Will Smith, for your music and a life that has inspired me to charge full steam at whatever I'm most afraid of.

And finally, to my parents, Carol and Steve. Thank you for all the sacrifices you made for us kids. I hope it was finally worth it.

INDEX

ABOUT THE AUTHOR

NOAH ST. JOHN, Ph.D., is Founder and CEO of **SuccessClinic.com**, an international success training company, and host of **WealthyFunTV**. Since 2005, he has influenced the lives of more than 350,000 people through his speaking and appearances. People and organizations in more than forty countries are using his breakthrough methods to get rid of their "head trash" and enjoy more control, freedom, and abundance in their lives and careers.

He is the author of *Permission to Succeed®* and *The Great Little Book of Afformations®*, which have been translated into four languages. Noah has appeared on CNN, ABC, NBC, CBS, and Fox News, and has been featured in *PARADE*, *Woman's Day*, *Modern Bride*, *Los Angeles Business Journal*, the *Chicago Sun-Times*, the *Washington Post*, *InStyle*, and *Selling Power*.

Noah's Students range from stay-at-home moms to industry-leading CEOs, schoolchildren to retirees. Thousands of people visit his daily movie blog **WealthyFunTV.com** to watch his latest adventures and experience first-hand his All-Access Pass into the new world he affectionately calls Self-Help 2.0.

Prior to becoming an internationally in-demand speaker and author, Noah worked as a waiter, secretary, retail salesperson, housekeeper, and professional ballet dancer. These experiences helped Noah realize that neither an expensive eduation nor "traditional success methods" hold the true key to success.

Fun fact: Noah once won an all-expenses-paid trip to Hawaii on the game show *Concentration* hosted by Alex Trebek, where he missed winning a new car by three seconds. (Note: he had not yet learned *The Secret Code of Success*.)